BLOODY B

HISTO

C000215360

# WINCHESTER

# BLOODY BRITISH HISTORY

## HISTORY

# WINCHESTER

**DON BRYAN, GERALDINE BUCHANAN, CLARE DIXON, JAMES KING**
WINCHESTER AREA TOURIST GUIDES ASSOCIATION

The History Press

First published in 2013

The History Press
The Mill, Brimscombe Port
Stroud, Gloucestershire, GL5 2QG
www.thehistorypress.co.uk

Reprinted 2015

British Library Cataloguing in Publication Data.
A catalogue record for this book is available from the British Library.

ISBN 978 0 7524 9326 8

Typesetting and origination by The History Press
Printed in Great Britain

# CONTENTS

# WINCHESTER

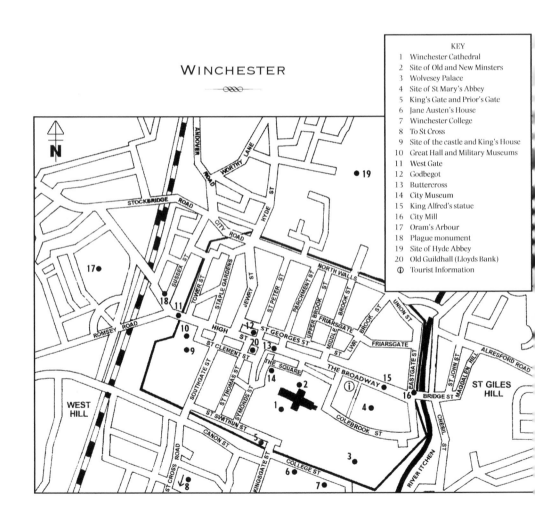

KEY

1 Winchester Cathedral
2 Site of Old and New Minsters
3 Wolvesey Palace
4 Site of St Mary's Abbey
5 King's Gate and Prior's Gate
6 Jane Austen's House
7 Winchester College
8 To St Cross
9 Site of the castle and King's House
10 Great Hall and Military Museums
11 West Gate
12 Godbegot
13 Buttercross
14 City Museum
15 King Alfred's statue
16 City Mill
17 Oram's Arbour
18 Plague monument
19 Site of Hyde Abbey
20 Old Guildhall (Lloyds Bank)
ⓘ Tourist Information

# INTRODUCTION

**T**HIS BOOK HAS been written by four members of the Winchester Area Tourist Guides Association, part of a professional team of qualified Blue and Green Badge Tourist Guides. Together we have many years of experience in guiding visitors around the Winchester area, lecturing to local groups and in some cases teaching courses on the History of Winchester. It is with delight that we accepted the invitation to write the edited highlights of this ancient capital's history.

Today Winchester is a fine place to live; streams of clear water run through it and there are some beautiful gardens. The medieval cathedral still flourishes and draws people from all over the world. Visitors, and indeed locals alike, are often unaware of the history that lies just beneath their feet.

The following chapters give some of the sordid, tragic or simply bizarre detail which underlies Winchester's development as the ancient capital of England, and its long history as a royal and religious power-house. If you would like to find out more, why not come on one of our tours? Details can be found at http://www.winchestertouristguides.com.

We would like to thank all our friends and colleagues, especially Tony Humphrys, Tony Newing, Martin McDonald Woods and the staffs of Winchester Museum Service, Southampton Museum Service, Winchester College, Winchester Tourism, the Hospital of St Cross and Winchester Cathedral for their support and advice. All royalties from sales of this book will be donated either to local or national charities including those supported by the Mayor of Winchester.

*Don Bryan*
*Geraldine Buchanan*
*Clare Dixon*
*James King*

# EARLY HISTORY

THE CITY OF Winchester lies in the valley of the River Itchen, a beautiful chalk stream that rises from springs near Cheriton, a few miles to the north-east. Ancient trackways, used for thousands of years by our ancestors, dropped down to cross a ford over the river. These ancient routes are still used as long-distance footpaths, and the approach to the ford is Winchester's modern High Street, making it one of the oldest streets in Britain.

It is in the area around this ford that an Iron Age tribe called the *Belgae* created a settlement to the west of the modern city, now called Oram's Arbour. It is thought that this enclosure was not a main habitation site but that the Iron Age farmers lived and worked in farmsteads scattered around on the chalk downland encircling Winchester. They may have used the settlement as a market, since when the Romans conquered the area they called their new city *Venta Belgarum*

*Winchester High Street. (Clare Dixon)*

– 'the market place of the Belgae people'. Under the Romans, Winchester grew to be one of the most important cities in Roman Britain, although there is virtually nothing left of their city above ground.

When The Brooks Shopping Centre was planned in the 1980s a large excavation was undertaken by the Winchester Museum Service and volunteers. During this excavation it was discovered that the Romans had physically moved the River Itchen from The Brooks area to where it flows today at The Weirs, to the east of Winchester. Huge timber drains were discovered during The Brooks excavation; these would have been used to drain the area for further expansion of the Roman city in the third century AD. It was at this time that a 3m-wide stone wall was built around the city, replacing earth ramparts and ditches.

Roman law forbade burial within the city, with the exception of infants, so that the dead did not physically or spiritually pollute the world of the living. The largest Roman cemetery is to the north-west of Winchester. It occupied the area between the Silchester and Cirencester Roman roads, now the Andover Road and Worthy Lane. Known as The Lankhills cemetery, it was one of the largest in southern Britain with hundreds of graves spanning the Roman period. Other smaller cemeteries surrounding the city have been recorded over the years.

When the Roman Army left Britain around AD 410 many of their cities became totally abandoned. This was the case with Winchester. The decay can be seen in archaeological levels across the city and may have continued for nearly 200 years, before a new people occupied

*Skeleton of an infant found in an Iron Age pit, Oram's Arbour. (Don Bryan)*

the area. These were the Saxons, one of many Northern European tribes who invaded Britain in the fifth century. According to legend, one of the last British kings, King Arthur, fought a rearguard action before being killed at the Battle of Camlan. A fifteenth-century writer places Camelot at Winchester, and of course we do have King Arthur's Round Table hanging in the Great Hall at Winchester.

Birinus, one of the missionaries who had followed St Augustine to England, arrived in Hamwic (Southampton) in 634. Not long after, a church was established at Winchester by King Cenwalh, his father King Cynegils having been baptised by Birinus in 635. Bishop Wine was appointed first Bishop of Winchester in 660 and in 678 the original missionary base was moved from Dorchester on Thames to Winchester.

Our knowledge of what happened in Winchester for the next 150 years is limited, but by 828 the Royal House of Wessex had been established by King Egbert, the grand-father of King Alfred. It is thanks to Alfred himself that our city became the capital of England.

# 849–899

# KING ALFRED: GREAT AGAINST VIKINGS

**T**HE ONLY ENGLISH king to be called 'Great', though he was never king of all England.

When Alfred was born in 849 in Wantage, in Berkshire, there were four kingdoms in England: Wessex, Northumbria, East Anglia and Mercia. At the time of his death in 899, Wessex was the only independent English kingdom left. The rest of the country was under the influence of the Vikings who had first raided Northumbria 100 years earlier.

The Vikings may have gone as traders to other parts of Europe but they came to England to attack and loot; Winchester was first attacked in 860. However, the Danish Great Army which arrived in 866 had a further objective. They were not just content to raid and go home with their booty and captives as winter approached: they were coming to invade and settle.

Alfred the Great was the youngest of five sons of King Æthelwulf of Wessex, who reigned from 839-848, so it was unlikely that he would ever become king. However, all four of his brothers died young – after three had already had a turn at being king. Surprisingly

for the time, none of their deaths seemed to have involved foul play by their youngest brother.

According to the Anglo-Saxon Chronicle, Alfred's first battle was in 868 when he and his brother, King Æthelred, came to Nottingham to assist the Mercians against the Danes. After Danish success against Northumbria and East Anglia in 870, Wessex itself was invaded. In that year Æthelred and Alfred fought nine battles. They were heavily defeated at Reading, after which the Danes set off westwards along the Great Ridgeway to make further inroads into Wessex. Here they were met by the Wessex army, at Ashdown near the Uffington White Horse in Berkshire. Alfred won victory by leading a ferocious charge uphill 'like a wild boar'. The Danes fled and after the battle 'the whole breadth of Ashdown was covered in bodies'.

However, there were further defeats ahead. Alfred's brother, King Æthelred, was seriously wounded at the Battle of Meredun (thought to be Merdon on the road to Romsey, 5 miles from Winchester). Alfred became king of Wessex when Æthelred died of his wounds a few weeks later, with a kingdom consisting of Kent, Sussex, Berkshire, Hampshire, Dorset, Wiltshire, Somerset and the lower Severn valley. The year 871 ended in defeat for the twenty-one-year-old king at Wilton in Wiltshire, but he was able to buy the Danes off and they turned to attack Mercia. However, Alfred knew that this would only be a temporary truce.

The Danes came back in 876 and again Alfred was able to force the Danish leader, Guthrun, to leave Wessex. Admittedly he had the help of the elements, as a Viking fleet was destroyed by a storm off Swanage in Dorset. In January 878, Guthrun made a sudden attack on Chippenham where Alfred was celebrating Twelfth Night, and Alfred was forced to flee to the Isle of Athelney in Somerset. This is where the eleventh-century story of Alfred burning the 'cakes' in a poor woman's hovel is based. Alfred was at the lowest point in his entire reign but seven weeks after Easter, with men summoned from Hampshire, Somerset and Wiltshire, he resoundingly defeated the Danes at Edington in Wiltshire. Guthrun was forced not only to agree to withdraw his army from Wessex, but also to become a Christian.

Alfred was not just a brave warrior and an effective war leader. Between 878 and 892, he reorganised the army on a shift system so that it could be permanently in the field, without as much impact on the working lives of individual part-time soldiers. Also, in an attempt to defeat the Vikings before they got to Wessex's shores, Alfred designed and commanded better and larger ships.

The military reform that had the most profound effect on Winchester was Alfred's creation of fortified towns with permanent garrisons. Where remnants of Roman walls already existed, as at Winchester, he repaired them. The hope was that these garrisons could hold any Viking incursion until the main army arrived. In his reign a new street plan was created for Winchester, using as the main axis the line of the old Iron Age trackway which had become the Roman High Street, as it still is. At right angles to the High Street, other roads were built at regular intervals in the direction of the north and south walls. Parallel service lanes were created behind the High Street on both sides. These can still be traced in St Clements's Lane and Market Lane on the south side, and George Street on the north. Alfred wanted his

*Hamo Thornycroft's statue of King Alfred the Great in The Broadway erected to commemorate the millennium of his death in 899. (Winchester Tourism)*

*Silver penny minted in Winchester, on display in the City Museum. Alfred's image is in the imperial style, based on the coinage of Emperor Charlemagne. (Winchester City Council Museums)*

fortified towns to become prosperous so they could contribute to the cost of armies and garrisons. In Winchester's case this prosperity was probably based on a growing consumer demand from the Church and presumably from frequent visits by the royal court, as well as a growing wool and cloth industry.

Whilst these reforms were being put into place, the years from 878 to 885 were, fortunately for Alfred and Wessex, relatively quiet. However, from 885 Alfred had to work hard to defend Wessex's eastern boundary from Danish attack, as the wide Thames estuary was a very tempting route for them. So he seized London in 886, then part of Mercia, but diplomatically left it in the charge of the Mercian ealdorman,

Æthelred, to whom he gave his daughter Æthelflaed in marriage.

This move against London resulted in yet another peace treaty with Guthrun. England was divided along the line of Watling Street between Wessex and the rest of England, now known as the Danelaw. Guthrun was in charge of the Danelaw but acknowledged Alfred as his overlord; a step in the direction of the Wessex monarchs becoming kings of all England.

Despite this agreement, there was intermittent fighting against many Danish leaders for the rest of Alfred's reign. According to the Anglo-Saxon Chronicle, after one attempted Danish attack in 896, 'The sea cast two ships on to the land, and the men were brought to Winchester to the king, and he ordered them to be hanged'. This is the only reference to the living Alfred ever being in Winchester, a town over which he had so much influence.

After Alfred died in 899, he was initially buried in Winchester's Old Minster and then re-interred in the new enlarged minster alongside, which was built to reflect the increased power of the Wessex kings. His work in defending and expanding Wessex's power was carried on by his son Edward the Elder and grandson, Æthelstan, who was the first monarch to be recognised as King of all England.

# c.863–1538

# ST SWITHUN'S RESTLESS BONES

**W**HO WAS ST Swithun? In modern times, he is seen as the unofficial patron saint of weather forecasters. If it rains on 15 July, it will rain for forty days, so folklore says.

Swithun was Bishop of Winchester from 840 until his death in around 863. He appears to have led a blameless and virtuous life, and may have been a tutor to the young Prince Alfred. He had the bridge over the River Itchen rebuilt. He is alleged to have made whole some eggs that a poor woman had dropped when crossing the new bridge, hence the adjacent pub is named Bishop on the Bridge.

It is what happened to his bones after his death that caused problems. He wanted to be buried in the graveyard outside the Old Minster, to be amongst the common folk, where people could walk over his tomb to show his humility. He got his wish and was buried outside the west door; however he was not to be left in peace.

Many miracles began to occur by his tomb; he seemed particularly to favour the lame and the blind. As the cult of the locally canonised St Swithun grew, it was felt in the next century that his body should be in a less humble position.

On 15 July 971, the saint's bones were taken out of his stone coffin, put into a temporary shrine and carried in solemn procession to the High Altar of the Old Minster. Wulfstan, a choir boy who went on to become one of the principal Anglo-Saxon poets, said that it poured with rain all day; the locals said it was the saint weeping in sorrow. This is the origin of the story that if it rains on 15 July it will rain for the next forty days. Miracles continued and his bones were not allowed to rest in peace or even to stay intact. In 974, the bones were disturbed

*Statue of a bishop, thought to be St Swithun, on top of the cathedral's west front. (James King)*

*Wall painting in Corhampton church showing a poor lady and Bishop Swithun on his new bridge, with her eggs falling from her basket between the two left-hand figures. (James King)*

again and split in two; part remained in a shrine on the High Altar, the rest were placed in a reliquary covered with gold, silver and gems. This was moved into a permanent shrine over his original burial site with a purpose-built chapel around it, in what had become part of the extended Old Minster.

It gets worse. When Bishop Alphage of Winchester became Archbishop of Canterbury in 1006, he took St Swithun's head with him to impress his new diocese. An arm may have gone to Peterborough. The reliquary containing the now headless collection of bones was given pride of place when the cathedral was rebuilt by the Normans, and in 1093 it was installed behind the High Altar.

Pilgrims could get close to the saint's bones and other holy relics by crawling into a 'Holy' Hole beneath them. In the twelfth century Reinhald, probably a Winchester monk, travelled to Norway, reputedly taking Swithun's other arm with him. The arm was placed in the new Stavanger Cathedral. Meanwhile in Canterbury, Alphage's successors, who had no links with Winchester, had lost interest in the saint's skull so somehow it ended up at Evreux in Normandy. The remaining relics at Winchester were moved again in 1476, when a new shrine was built in the retrochoir behind the High Altar. Finally when that shrine was demolished in Henry VIII's reign in 1538, the remaining bones were scattered.

The site of Swithun's original grave is now marked by a modern stone slab, given by Stavanger Cathedral, to the left of the west-front of the cathedral. Would reuniting St Swithun's bones today improve the quality of our summers?

# 985–1052

# QUEEN EMMA WHIPS THE KING!

OR ALMOST 100 years after the death of King Alfred, his successors continued the expansion of the West Saxon kingdom and consolidated England's nationhood. The House of Wessex reached its zenith with the coronation of Alfred's great-grandson Edgar in 973. The nation was growing in prosperity and stature and the Danes had been subdued.

It was Edgar's son, Æthelred 'The Unready', who turned triumph to disaster for England. It was this Æthelred that married the very beautiful Emma, 'the pearl of Normandy'.

In the High Street, near Winchester's City Cross, stands a building called 'God Begot House'. The present building, heavily restored, dates to the sixteenth century. It has been used for a variety of purposes and today is a popular restaurant. This area of Winchester was once a Royal Manor, which in the year 1012 was given by King Æthelred to his wife Emma. They had been married at Canterbury Cathedral in 1002, and in 1003 a son was born. He was to become Edward the Confessor, King of England.

It was here at God Begot that Emma had a two-storey house built, which became her home in Winchester. It may have been in this house that Emma gave birth to a second son, Alfred, in 1013.

These were troubled times as the Viking army was in England, attacking many towns. This force was under the control of Sweyn and his son Canute. The Royal Family were forced to leave England in 1014 but returned later that year. Æthelred died just two years later and Canute married Emma. In 1019 Emma gave birth to another boy, Hardecanute, the son of Canute. Hardecanute took precedence over Æthelred's sons, Edward and Alfred, who at this time were in Normandy.

In 1035 Canute died and his son Hardecanute became king briefly, until he too died, so the crown went to Edward the Confessor. After he became king, Edward appears to have had little confidence in his mother, probably because she favoured the children of her second husband instead of supporting Edward's claim to the throne. What follows is a summary of the legend surrounding Emma some years after the death of both her husbands.

Robert, Archbishop of Canterbury, persuaded Edward the Confessor that

*God Begot House is built on the site of Queen Emma's manor. (James King)*

his mother had been guilty of too close a relationship with Alwine, Bishop of Winchester. This was despite Alwine having been dead for three years!

As a result of this accusation, most of Emma's land was confiscated and she was sent to Wherwell Priory near Andover in North Hampshire.

She was not very strictly confined there and was at liberty to write to certain bishops whom she trusted, saying she was far more shocked at the scandal surrounding Alwine than at the allegations made against her. She said she was even willing to submit to the ordeal of burning iron in order to prove the bishop's innocence. The bishops surrounding the king advised him to let the trial by ordeal go ahead, but the archbishop felt that this was not

enough. He wanted Emma to make a double purgation in order to prove both her innocence and that of the bishop. He advised the king that she should walk over four burning ploughshares for herself and five for the bishop in order to prove their innocence. Preparations were made accordingly and Emma spent the night beforehand in prayer at the shrine of St Swithun in the Old Minster at Winchester, where the 'ordeal of burning iron' would take place. The saint appeared before her and said, 'I am St Swithun whom you have invoked; fear not, the fire shall do you no hurt.'

The next day the king assembled with his court to watch his mother submit to the ordeal. The nine ploughshares were made red hot and placed on the pavement in the church. Then Emma entered the church and made a long invocation which began, 'Oh God, who didst save Susannah from the malice of the wicked elders, save me!' She then trod on the glowing metal with her bare feet but felt nothing. She asked the bishops who were leading her by the hand to tell her when they came to the ploughshares. They told her that she had already passed over them. Her feet were examined and found to be uninjured.

The king was then convinced of her innocence and repented his cruelty. He fell at his mother's feet, saying 'Mother, I have sinned before heaven and before you.'

He was whipped by both the bishops and his mother. Emma's property was restored to her and the archbishop was banished.

After the Normans had built their cathedral the bones of various Kings of England, along with certain relics and the bones of Bishop Alwine and Queen

Emma, were moved into the newly constructed cathedral. These bones were eventually put together in boxes called 'mortuary chests' which can still be seen in Winchester Cathedral, on top of the early sixteenth-century presbytery screen of the choir.

Some of these mortuary chests were brought down from their resting places by Parliamentarian soldiers when they ransacked the cathedral in 1642. After they left the bones were collected up, so it may well be that Emma and her Bishop Alwine have ended up in the same chest!

These mortuary chests have been opened and their contents examined, described, drawn and photographed on several occasions since. To bring the story up to date, in 2012 the cathedral authorities received permission for some of the human remains to be scientifically examined and analysed using DNA technology. It will be interesting to learn what conclusions are reached.

# 1066–1100

# DISPATCHED IN HASTINGS

**A**T THE START of 1066 Winchester was the principal city of Saxon southern England, home to the Royal Palace, Royal Treasure House and Mint. In 1051 the heirless Edward the Confessor offered the English throne to Duke William of Normandy on his death. This offer was confirmed in 1064 with a visit by Harold Godwinson, on behalf of the king, to William in Normandy.

There was considerable support for William's claim to the throne, so when Harold declared himself King of England on Edward's death, William felt obliged to act. In 1066 he raised an invasion force and landed near Hastings where he fought and killed Harold at the famous battle outside the present-day Sussex town of Battle.

There were at this time three major monastic foundations in Winchester. Old Minster, with strongly Norman sympathies, had been staffed with Benedictine monks from the Abbey of Fleury in Normandy since the tenth century. The monastery of New Minster and the nunnery known as the Nunnaminster supported the English point of view. All three minsters played

## LADY EDITH

Edward the Confessor's widow, Edith or Eadgyth, appears to have sympathised with William. She lived in Winchester and was reputedly the richest woman in England at the time. On the death of her mother-in-law, Queen Emma, Edith had assumed the title of 'the Lady'. Guy of Amiens in his poem on the Conquest says: 'William sent to Guincestre, and bade the chief men, as others did, bring tribute to him; the chief men conferred with the Lady Edith and she consented and bade them bear the tribute; and so all came in to it, and the messengers carried back the gifts of the Lady and those of the chief men also'. It has been suggested that she was an instigator of the Bayeux Tapestry, knowing well of the skills of the Nunnaminster nuns.

*A fragment of the Bayeux Tapestry possibly made by the nuns of the Nunnaminster. (THP)*

their separate parts as Norman rule replaced the Saxon way of life.

Monks from the New Minster, led by Abbot Ælfwig – Harold's uncle – joined Harold's army to fight against William at Hastings, whilst the monks of the Old Minster quietly stayed at home in Winchester. The Bayeux Tapestry was commissioned in the 1070s, probably by Odo of Bayeux, half-brother of Duke William, and the nuns of Nunnaminster may have had a hand in making it. It tells the story of the events leading up to William's invasion and is one of the great treasures of France. Odo was deeply unpopular in England and his role in preparing the invasion, shown in the tapestry, is probably an exaggeration, but his side won and it is the victorious who write the history; hence the very Norman slant displayed at Bayeux!

Winchester was still a seat of royal power, so it was to Winchester that William sent to secure the Royal Treasure House and Mint immediately following his coronation at Westminster, which had been conducted by Bishop Ealdred of York, a former monk of Old Minster.

William made Winchester his headquarters as it was well placed to reach Rouen – his power base in Normandy – as well as London. Initially he nearly doubled the size of the Saxon Royal Palace at the expense of the precinct of the New Minster – revenge perhaps for their opposition at Hastings. Then in 1070 construction of Winchester Castle began on a raised site in the south-west corner of the Roman city walls. By around 1100 the castle was complete, combining the functions of royal residence, treasure house and fortress.

Bishop Stigand had become Archbishop of Canterbury in 1052, and was at the same time Bishop of Winchester, but by 1066 had been excommunicated by the Pope. He had been Earl Godwin's friend, and had taken Harold's side at Hastings. To William he was too strong an Anglo-Saxon bishop to be left in possession of either Winchester or Canterbury and so, though he submitted to William, he was taken as a hostage to Normandy. Soon after he

*Statue of Earl Waltheof on the ruined west front of Croyland Abbey, Lincolnshire. Waltheof was the only Saxon nobleman to be executed by the Normans. (Geraldine Buchanan)*

escaped to Scotland, but in 1072 he again fell into William's hands. He was brought to Winchester as a prisoner and was kept under guard in the castle until his death later that year. He lies buried somewhere in Winchester Cathedral.

About the same time a bloody episode occurred at Winchester which produced a popular English saint of the age. Waltheof was the second son of Siward, Earl of Northumberland – a Dane who had risen to prominence under King Cnut. In 1055 Waltheof was considered too young to inherit the earldom, with responsibility for defending the North of England against invasions from Scotland, Denmark and Sweden. Instead King Edward the Confessor made him earl of several midland counties and made Harold's brother, Tostig, Earl of Northumberland. Although Waltheof attended the Royal Court in 1068, in 1069 he became involved in the plot to put Edgar Ætheling on the throne in place of William, but then gave himself up at York, begging forgiveness and swearing another oath of allegiance. In 1070 Waltheof was at the council in Winchester and in high favour, and in 1072 he finally received his father's title of Earl of Northumberland.

Waltheof misread William's generosity as weakness, and in 1075 got embroiled in another plot with Earl Ralph of Norfolk and the Earl of Hereford. Waltheof controlled land between their two territories, and if all three colluded they could have commanded enough of the country to threaten William. For being part of this conspiracy, William had Waltheof imprisoned for five months at Winchester before having him condemned to death for treason. Waltheof was to be executed at dawn on St Petronilla's Day, 31 May 1076. Early that morning he gave all his valuables including his clothes to the poor and was taken up St Giles Hill, east of Winchester, to be executed almost in secret. He begged to be allowed to say the Lord's Prayer one last time before he was beheaded; permission was given but when he reached '... and lead us not into temptation ...' he hesitated, sobbing. The executioner got impatient and the axe fell, but the few people present believed they heard the final Latin words '... but deliver us from evil, Amen' after the head had been severed.

Waltheof was the only high-born Englishman executed by William. He became a hero of the Anglo-Saxon resistance, and was later buried in the Chapter House of Croyland Abbey in Lincolnshire. In 1092, after a fire in the Chapter House, the abbot had Waltheof's body moved to a prominent place in the abbey church. When the coffin was opened, the corpse was found to be intact with the severed head re-joined to the neck. This was regarded as a miracle, and the abbey capitalised on it. Pilgrims began to visit Waltheof's tomb, and healing miracles were reputed to occur there.

# 1100

# MURDER MOST FOUL?

## THE DEATH OF WILLIAM RUFUS

History shows that powerful kings often had troublesome children; this was true for William the Conqueror. We know that his son, William II, was buried in 1100 in what was then the newly completed Norman cathedral at Winchester. But how did he die? The suspicion is that he was murdered by – or at least on the orders of – his brother, Henry.

William II, called Rufus because of his red hair and ruddy complexion, was not a popular king. William the Conqueror had four sons: the eldest, Robert, succeeded his father as Duke of Normandy. The next, Richard, was killed by a stag whilst hunting in the New Forest and was buried in Winchester Cathedral. William Rufus, the third son, inherited the throne of England on his father's death in 1087. There were many who would have preferred Robert as king. Rufus failed to reward even those barons who did support him, and alienated the Church to such a degree that the Pope was considering his excommunication. The youngest brother, Henry, felt overlooked and

may well have seen an opportunity to advance his own interests.

On 2 August 1100 William Rufus was out hunting in the New Forest 20 miles from Winchester. One version of the story goes that he had been drinking heavily the night before and so did not set out until the afternoon with,

*Walter Tyrrell makes good his escape ... one version of the legend. (THP)*

most unusually, just one attendant: Walter Tyrrell, well known for his skill as an archer. William's younger brother, Henry, was also hunting with another, larger party. William had just dismounted when Walter, trying to show off, shot hurriedly at a stag; the arrow glanced off an oak tree and hit William in the chest, killing him instantly. Walter fled to Poole, crossing the River Avon at a place now called Avon Tyrrell. Here legend says he stopped at a blacksmith's shop to have the shoes on his horse's hooves reversed in order to confuse pursuers. He reached the safety of France and never returned to England. We should note that he later swore to his friend Sergerius, Abbot of St Denis at Paris, that he had never even seen the king in the forest that day.

There was no pursuit. Popular legend says that William's body was eventually found by a charcoal burner called Purkiss, who took it on his cart to the royal city of Winchester for burial. Meanwhile Henry, with a suspicious speed suggesting that he had fast horses ready and waiting, had also returned to Winchester to claim the Treasury of England held at the castle. He was challenged by the Keeper of the Treasury, William of Breteuil, who reminded Henry of his oath that his brother Robert should inherit the crown of England. Conveniently for Henry, Robert was away on Crusade at this time. Henry, drawing his sword, declared that 'he would suffer no upstart to cause ill found delay in seizing his father's sceptre before he could'. He hurried on to London and was crowned Henry I on 6 August, just four days after William Rufus' death. He even got the girl! Rufus

## DIVINE DISPLEASURE?

When the tower of Winchester Cathedral collapsed over his burial place just six years later, contemporaries felt this proved that there was something 'not right' about the life and death of William Rufus. Such a disaster must be the result of Divine displeasure. To the modern mind it is more likely a result of the great Norman cathedral having been built at amazing speed (in less than twenty years). The rough placing of the original stones and mortar can still be seen, in clear contrast to the slower, more careful work in rebuilding the tower afterwards. Many visitors remark on the rather squat nature of the cathedral's tower today – it's all that the medieval builders dared to put up as a replacement to a structure which, who knows, may once have been much more splendid and commanding.

had previously visited Romsey Abbey (12 miles from Winchester) to woo Edith, daughter of King Malcolm of Scotland, who was being educated in the nunnery there. Her aunt Christina, the Abbess, had pretended that Edith was a nun to protect her from his attentions. However, Henry was clearly more to Edith's liking and she married him soon after his coronation.

So how about Rufus's bones? For many years they were thought to lie in a Purbeck marble tomb before the High Altar of Winchester Cathedral. At this early date effigies were not used on tombs, and there is no trace of an inscription. The tomb was opened in 1868 and the local paper, the *Hampshire*

*The Rufus Stone claims to mark the position of the oak tree off which the arrow glanced before hitting William Rufus. The original stone was set up in the eighteenth century 'by John Lord Delaware who had seen the tree growing in this place'. The present memorial, enclosing Delaware's stone, dates from 1841. (Clare Dixon)*

*Chronicle*, reported, 'some curious things were found' including 'part of a metallic rod, possibly part of the very arrow which slew the king'. These days, however, the tomb is considered more likely to be that of Henri de Blois, an eminent bishop of the twelfth century. It is possible that the bones of William Rufus are in two of the cathedral's six mortuary chests, as the seventeenth-century inscriptions on their sides claim. Current DNA testing may shed some light.

In the meantime, Rufus has a memorial near Canterton in the New Forest, where the Rufus Stone marks the spot where he died (fittingly, the nearby pub is the Walter Tyrrell). But even that is the subject of controversy – there is also a Rufus Memorial Cairn in the gardens of Beaulieu Abbey, some miles away, which makes the same claim!

# 1100–1135

# DROWNING AND DISMEMBERMENTS

**K**ING HENRY I and Matilda, formerly known as Edith, had two legitimate children, Matilda born in 1102 and William born in 1103. Henry had at least twenty illegitimate children including Robert, later Earl of Gloucester.

In the year their daughter Matilda was born, a fire broke out in the centre of Winchester which destroyed a large part of the city including the Royal Palace, the Mint and the Guildhall, along with several dwellings around what is now the city museum. Many ancient records were also destroyed at this time.

The project to rebuild the cathedral tower in 1107, after its collapse, was one of several elements of friction growing between the monks of New Minster and their neighbours, both monastic and royal. In 1110 this led to the relocation of New Minster, which was originally just to the north of the present cathedral, to a district north of the city called Hyde. The new Hyde Abbey was very spacious and may have been one of the five largest abbeys in England.

For some reason Winchester was not included in the Domesday Book survey compiled by the monks of Winchester in 1086 – perhaps an early attempt at tax-evasion? However in 1110, King Henry I gave instructions that a new survey should be carried out at Winchester which would list the royal holdings in the city. This became known as the *Liber Winton*. This survey showed that Winchester was one of the largest cities in England with an estimated 1,300 houses, making it second only to London. It was during this period that the city was at the height of its medieval development, with an ambitious building programme both within the city at the cathedral and at Wolvesey Palace, the residence of the Bishops of Winchester.

Relationships between the king and certain residents of Winchester were not always as close as they could have been. Henry was a very stern man and gave out severe punishment where he thought fit. Such a case happened in 1118 when one of his treasury staff, Henry the Camerarius, was blinded and castrated for irregularities in Treasury affairs.

This severe nature of King Henry became apparent after the Royal Palace and Mint were rebuilt following the disastrous fire of 1102. Henry took advantage of the new Mint to stop the

*Drowning of Prince William on the* White Ship, *1120. (Cassell's History of England)*

corrupt moneyers 'clipping' the coins for silver and making quite a fortune from this illegal act. Roger, Bishop of Sarum, advised the king that he should assemble the moneyers from all over the country at Winchester to inspect their coins. So at Christmas 1125 they gathered at Winchester and their coins were rigorously examined for 'clipping'. Those moneyers found guilty received severe punishment as the Anglo-Saxon Chronicle for the year 1125 records:

> When they came thither, they were seized one by one, and each deprived of the right hand and the testicles below. All this was done within the Twelvenight, and it was all with great justice, because they had ruined all the land with their great fraud, they bought all that dearly.

At the same time Henry also stopped the practice of selling short, which is selling cloth below the accepted measure. He introduced a standard yard that would be held at Winchester so that cloth could be measured against it at any time. Any merchant found not conforming to this standard yard was punished.

An event occurred in 1120 that would eventually lead to the destruction of large parts of Winchester and one of the darkest episodes in the city's history.

On 25 November 1120 two ships left the port of Barfleur in Normandy. The first ship to leave carried King Henry I. The second ship, *la Blanche-Nef* (the *White Ship*) was owned by Thomas FitzStephen whose father had carried William the Conqueror to England in 1066. The 300 passengers included William, the seventeen-year-old son and only legitimate male heir of King Henry. The crew had been celebrating the marriage of William and his new bride Matilda and vast quantities of wine were consumed. The crew, being very drunk, attempted to leave the port but hit rocks just outside the harbour and all but one were drowned. The young William was one of the victims along with several members of the royal household. When told of the disaster Henry was overcome with grief and some say he never smiled again.

King Henry I died in December 1135 after eating a 'surfeit of lampreys'. He was buried in Reading Abbey and the dark cloud of civil war hung over Winchester.

*King Henry I. (THP)*

# 1135–1154

# TWO MATILDAS, ONE COUNTRY

**W**HEN PRINCE WILLIAM drowned in 1120, Henry's daughter became his only surviving heir. In 1110 this eight-year-old girl had left England to marry Emperor Henry V of Germany, and became the Empress Matilda.

After Prince William's death, King Henry arranged for the barons to swear oaths that on his death Empress Matilda would become Queen of England. But when he died in 1135, despite their sworn oaths, the barons offered the crown to Stephen, grandson of William the Conqueror. Stephen had conveniently avoided boarding the *White Ship*, being struck down with diarrhoea just before the ship sailed. After initial opposition Stephen was welcomed in London where he was crowned in

*Emperor Henry V of Germany and Matilda's wedding feast. (THP)*

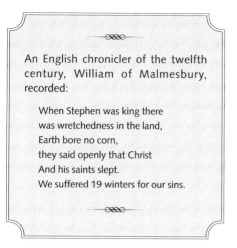

An English chronicler of the twelfth century, William of Malmesbury, recorded:

When Stephen was king there
was wretchedness in the land,
Earth bore no corn,
they said openly that Christ
And his saints slept.
We suffered 19 winters for our sins.

Westminster Abbey on 22 December 1135 – after first securing the Treasury at Winchester. This coronation triggered nineteen years of civil war between King Stephen and Empress Matilda, and brought disaster to England.

By early 1139 various towns and castles were under siege, and Stephen had arrested the Bishops of Salisbury, Lincoln and Ely. These arrests infuriated his brother, Henri de Blois, Bishop of Winchester, and one of the most powerful men in the land. Bishop Henri summoned a synod to Winchester to discuss the matter.

In September 1139, the empress landed in Sussex and her forces were besieged at Arundel Castle but eventually Bishop Henri arranged safe passage for her and her retinue to Bristol. Stephen was captured at the Battle of Lincoln in February 1141 and brought before the empress at Gloucester before being confined in Bristol Castle.

The empress was invited to a Great Conference in Oxford at Easter 1141 where she was accepted by the Church as the heir of King Henry. Triumphal processions followed at Oxford, Wilton

and Reading and finally, on 3 March 1141 she entered Winchester in procession. At the West Gate, throngs of supporters watched her pass down the High Street to enter the cathedral precinct. So many people were present that some climbed up the cathedral to get a better view, dislodging stones which fell on those below. The empress entered the cathedral with Bishop Henri de Blois on her right hand, and the Bishop of St David's on her left, with the Bishops of Ely and Lincoln in support. Empress Matilda was declared 'Lady of the English', and recognised by Theobald, Archbishop of Canterbury when he arrived in Winchester a few days later. The empress moved to Westminster in June 1141 in preparation for her coronation as Queen of England, but during the few days she was there she totally alienated the citizens by demanding heavy taxes from them.

Just to confuse matters, King Stephen's wife was also called Matilda;

*Empress Matilda's escape in the snow. (THP)*

29

she was known as Queen Matilda. Her pleas for the release of Stephen from Bristol were ignored, so she raised an army in Kent and headed towards London. When her army reached the capital the citizens of London rang church bells as an alarm and then let the queen's army in and offered support to her against the empress.

The empress left Westminster and rode to Oxford, where Bishop Henri de Blois deserted her. He returned to Winchester, where he fortified his palace at Wolvesey.

On 31 July 1141 the empress entered Winchester with her troops and took control of the castle. She besieged Wolvesey Palace but Bishop Henri had already left. The next day the queen arrived with her army outside Winchester and surrounded it preventing all provisions entering the city.

In the next few days half the city was destroyed by fire and the empress was forced back inside the castle. Perhaps as many as twenty-three churches were burnt, damaged and looted. St Mary's Abbey and possibly Hyde Abbey were fired. The old Royal Palace and the area around St Lawrence's church were destroyed. The queen's army also sacked homes and shops, taking away spoil and captives. The empress fled Winchester on 14 September and headed west pursued by the queen's forces. At Stockbridge, 9 miles from Winchester, Robert of Gloucester, the empress's half-brother, fought a rearguard action to allow the empress to cross the River Test, but was himself captured by the queen's army.

In October 1141 a treaty was signed at Winchester whereby King Stephen was exchanged for Robert of Gloucester, leading to a further stalemate.

The empress retreated to Oxford and sent for the support of her new husband, the Count of Anjou. This eventually arrived in fifty-two ships carrying 300 knights and the empress's son, the young Prince Henry. Meanwhile Stephen attacked Oxford and laid siege to the castle, trapping the empress inside. She made a daring escape, crossing the frozen River Thames in the snow, camouflaged by white gowns.

The Civil War continued but in 1147 Robert of Gloucester died and the empress retreated to Normandy in the spring of 1148, never to return to England.

For the next five years the country remained in a state of turmoil and famine. In May 1152, Stephen's wife, Queen Matilda, died. In January 1153, Prince Henry, now Duke of Normandy, landed in England with 140 knights and 3,000 mercenaries. The armies of Prince Henry and King Stephen clashed inconclusively at Lincoln, Wallingford and Winchester.

Stephen's son Eustace was heir apparent to the throne of England, but 'he was an evil man and did more harm than good wherever he went'. He died suddenly in August 1153, allegedly struck down by the wrath of God while plundering Church lands near Bury St Edmunds. The death of Stephen's wife and then his son left him alone and vulnerable, and Bishop Henri de Blois made himself a mediator between the young Prince Henry and Stephen. To restore peace the Treaty of Winchester determined that when Stephen died, Prince Henry, the son of Empress Matilda, would become king.

Following Stephen's death in 1154, on 19 December Henry II was crowned King of England and peace returned at last.

# 1199–1272

# THE TROUBLESOME REIGNS OF JOHN AND HENRY III

JOHN, WHO BECAME king in 1199, was the youngest son of Henry II. Henry had controlled his family and his territory in England and France by the method of divide and rule. Not surprisingly, Prince John grew up to be an unscrupulous, untrustworthy, cruel and greedy monarch. It is highly likely that he murdered his nephew Arthur of Brittany in 1203, who, it could be argued, had a better claim to the throne than he did. John had an insatiable desire to accumulate wealth, especially as most of his money was spent fruitlessly on wars in France (where he failed to keep Normandy in the possession of the English Crown) and in Wales and Ireland.

King John never stayed more than a month at any one place. However, he did visit Winchester several times in 1207. According to the chronicler, Matthew Paris, John summoned the chief men of his kingdom for the purpose of extracting money. They were ordered to pay $^1/_{13}$ of their income. Whilst in Winchester, John set in place a system of further taxes on the Jews and followed that up with brutal methods of enforcing payment. Later in 1207, his queen, Isabella, gave birth in Winchester Castle to a son, Henry, who was to follow him as king. The baby was christened in Winchester Cathedral, probably in the Tournai marble font, one of the cathedral's treasures and where christenings still take place.

One of the more dramatic events of John's reign took place in Winchester in 1213. He had fallen out with Pope Innocent III who then placed John's kingdom under an interdict in 1208. That meant no one could be baptised, married, have a funeral service in a church or be buried in consecrated land. In retaliation, John confiscated all clerical property, and ordered the arrest of priests' mistresses, though he soon allowed them to purchase their freedom. (After all, it had only been in 1123 that priests had been stopped from marrying.) Pope Innocent followed up by excommunicating John in 1209. In political terms this meant John's throne could be seized by anyone strong enough. However, John's income from vacant Church posts was so great, that for the time being he preferred being excommunicated. But by 1213 John was increasingly surrounded by threats at home and from abroad, and, however

*Norman arches of the Chapter House through which King John entered with the bishops and barons in 1213. (Winchester City Council Museums)*

humiliating for him, he had no choice but to accept the Pope's demands with the negotiations ending at Winchester.

The exiled Archbishop of Canterbury, Stephen Langton, several other exiled bishops and a great number of barons came to Winchester. John went out to meet them on the road from London over Magdalen Hill, where he fell upon his knees and shed many tears. According to the chronicler, this had the effect of melting the whole company, who mingled their tears with his. The bishops raised him from the ground and all proceeded to the cathedral. This they could not enter as the king was still excommunicated so they convened in the Chapter House, now a ruin lying next to the cathedral, entering through the still standing Norman arches. Here the king renewed his coronation oath and promised to maintain the ancient laws of England. In return, he was absolved from his excommunication.

Inevitably, John did not keep his solemnly sworn oaths – even those in Magna Carta in 1215 – which provoked some barons into asking Prince Louis, son of Philip II of France, to be king. Prince Louis landed in Kent in 1216 and was able to enter London where he was proclaimed king. He captured Winchester Castle in June after a two-week siege. Few now seem to remember this French invasion and that for many months eastern and south-eastern England was under the rule of a French King of England. The crisis only ended with John's death in 1216 and Winchester Castle was recaptured in 1217 on behalf of the nine-year-old Henry III.

## WINCHESTER – CRIME HOTSPOT 1249

Faced with two merchants of Brabant complaining they had been robbed of 200 marks near the city of Winchester, Henry III in 1249 is said to have assembled his counsellors in Winchester who told him that, 'The neighbourhood of Winchester is infamous throughout the kingdom for the robberies, violence and murders committed there upon strangers; that the judges and magistrates have in vain attempted to eradicate this evil, because the juries in general are accomplices of the persons accused; that the great number of strangers, particularly from foreign parts, who flock to this city from the neighbouring port of Southampton, partly on account of the court being kept in it, partly on account of the great fairs which are held here, is a constant source of temptation to the ill-disposed.'

The king is said to have added, 'there is not a part of the country in such bad repute for robberies and murders as is this city, with its suburbs and neighbourhood. I am witness to them myself, and sufferer by them. My wine is openly and triumphantly carried away from the carts, whilst they are conveying it to my castle. I am quite ashamed of the city from which I derive my birth'.

When another jury failed to denounce the guilty parties, the king, in his frustration, imprisoned them in the castle dungeon. The next jury found them guilty. Even though many fled, some seeking sanctuary in churches, more than thirty were hanged with thirty more in prison fearing the same fate. Amongst the culprits were some of the king's own household who alleged that they had been driven to these bad courses through the fault of the king himself, in neglecting to pay them their just wages.

*Castle vault, Southampton where Henry III's wine would have been stored en route to Winchester. (Southampton City Council)*

Henry III felt some affinity with Winchester, where he had been born. He spent eighteen Christmases here in his fifty-six-year reign. Indeed in 1265, at the Battle of Evesham, he is reported to have said, 'I am Henry of Winchester your king, do not kill me'. In his reign the castle was extensively remodelled and the magnificent Great Hall was built, and still survives today. As a king, he was not much better than his father. He came to rely on foreign favourites, such as his young half-brother Aymer de Valence who, in 1250, he made Bishop of Winchester at the age of twenty-two, when he was not even ordained. Aymer was unpopular with the monks of Winchester and with the barons, both because of his financial exploitations and because he was foreign. This forced him into exile. He died abroad in 1260 but his heart came back to be buried in Winchester Cathedral.

*Looking through the Prior's Gate towards Kingsgate, c. 1915. (Winchester City Council Museums)*

Simon de Montfort had emerged as the leader of the dissatisfied English barons. In 1262, when Henry III was at Winchester to spend Whitsuntide, he refused to accept the barons' choices of Lord Chancellor and Lord Chief Justice. This provoked open war. The barons laid siege to Winchester hoping to capture the king, but he had left in the nick of time. Winchester soon surrendered and was sacked, with many of the inhabitants ill-treated and even killed. In 1264 tensions between different groups in the city led to an attack on the cathedral priory through the Prior's Gate.

This resulted in the burning down not only of that gate but also the nearby Kingsgate, with the church of St Swithun above it, and all the houses adjoining. The rioters also killed any of the priory servants that they could lay their hands on. In spring 1265, Winchester was again sacked, this time by de Montfort's son en route to help his father, but he failed to join him in time. De Montfort senior was killed at the Battle of Evesham in 1265. This meant the king was able to keep personal control of his kingdom until his death in 1272.

Despite Henry's affiliation with Winchester, its decline in importance was to become more marked in his reign. The Royal Mint was removed from Winchester in 1243 and the city suffered from much destruction in the war between the king and the barons. When Henry III died in 1272 he was buried in Westminster Abbey, which he had greatly enhanced. This became the future mausoleum of English monarchs.

## c. 1300

# GRIME DOESN'T PAY

**T**HE **MEDIEVAL HISTORY** of England is usually the story of kings, queens and the aristocracy, but in Winchester we are very fortunate to know something of the life of the city's ordinary inhabitants – in all its smelly, noisy reality. Winchester in 1300 had a population of perhaps 12,000, its prosperity based on wool and cloth. Allow us to introduce you to four of them: a rich merchant, a fuller, a laundress and someone who worked at the public latrines.

Archaeological excavations led by a team from the Winchester Museums

*'Middle Brook Street looking south' by S. Prout. This 1813 picture shows the street, with its open stream and timber-framed houses, much as it would have looked in medieval times. (Winchester City Council Museums)*

Service began in The Brooks area of Winchester in 1987 when the site was about to be developed as The Brooks Shopping Centre. The area is named after the three brooks, or open streams, which ran down the centre of the streets now known as Upper Brook Street, Middle Brook Street and Lower Brook Street (in fact the streams are still there today, though invisible in culverts under the road surface). In a ground-breaking study, information gained through this archaeological 'dig' was painstakingly linked to surviving documents to give us a glimpse – not only of medieval life in general, but of some named individuals.

John de Tyting was a successful merchant with a substantial property on Upper Brook Street, in which he probably lived from 1299 until his death in 1312. We know that he exported wool and supplied cloth to the royal household, was a Member of Parliament, and Mayor of Winchester in 1299 and again in 1305. His property covered two plots, with two shops fronting onto the street. He had a hall with a solar or private room and chapel leading off and also a private indoor lavatory – of which more anon! A rear yard was accessed through a large gate from the street and provided a warehouse, stabling and storage. Despite this being an urban house, he also enjoyed an orchard and gardens. His wealth and status are shown by finds that included part of a jet cross (perhaps from a pilgrimage to Spain), a piece of stained glass, and a walnut wood

## EXAMINING EXCREMENT

You can tell a lot about someone from what they eat, and fascinating information about the lives of John de Tyting and Stephen was found in their two latrines – John's private one with the wooden seat, and Stephen's in an old dovecot. From these we know that they both ate meat, although Stephen's was from older animals while John's included 'game' – such as boar and mallard – reserved for the privileged classes. John's food was spiced with caraway, coriander, dill and parsley. There is very little trace of vegetables in either of their diets, but John could afford a good range of fruit: fig, apple, mulberry, cherry, plum, strawberry and pear. The only fruit for Stephen was apple and blackberry, picked from the hedgerows.

Two jugs and a tankard, made in France, had been dropped into John's latrine. These may have been to hold water (there was no toilet paper in those days) or so that he could monitor his health by examining the colour of his urine. Perhaps the most striking aspect of John's latrine was the enormous number of parasitical worms' eggs – the penalty of a rich man's diet.

*John de Tyting's lavatory seat, discovered during The Brooks archaeological 'dig'. (Don Bryan)*

lavatory seat which can still be seen in the Winchester City Museum.

One of de Tyting's neighbours, from whom he also bought (unknown) services, was called Stephen. He was at the other extreme of the social spectrum, and city records mention him in connection with the Maiden Chamber or public latrines, situated just off the High Street – at the back of what is now Marks & Spencers. Here the upper and middle brooks join together and could be used to help wash away the waste, although urine had its uses, for example in tanning and fulling, and was probably collected – perhaps by Stephen. Stephen seems to have been an object of charity, receiving annual payments from the rents of two neighbours in Middle Brook Street, and from a local priest.

Backing on to John de Tyting was a more typical city plot, 40m long but only 9m wide, an arrangement which allowed as many businesses as possible to have a street frontage. Here, in a workshop at the rear separated from the house by a gravel yard, a stone-lined tank was found containing traces of fullers earth. Fulling was a smelly process, often involving the use of stale urine to help remove grease from woollen cloth; our modern noses wrinkle at the thought of a drain running from the tank into the middle brook. Documents tell us that by 1417 the fuller living there was called John Newman.

The final person to introduce is a laundress called Juliana, an upstream neighbour of John de Tyting, who appeared in a legal case against him in 1299. She argued John prevented her from washing clothes in the public stream and took her case to King Edward I at Winchester Castle. The king gave a landmark ruling in what has come to be known as the Concord de Julianne, 'water has always been common'. The Concord became a legal precedent, passing into English Common Law and from there to the UN Convention on Human Rights. Unexpected fame for a medieval laundress from Winchester! She too made use of urine, to wash clothes, and a big vat for holding it was found by archaeologists on the site of her house.

## GUTS IN THE RIVER!

Edward I's ruling said that water is common to all provided that they do not pollute it; for example with refuse of woad, hides from tanning, dung of men or animals or guts of animals; do not wash children's clothes with their filth; nor have garderobes or drains over it. What a vivid picture of a medieval city! But the authorities did their best. The city butchers in particular were regularly fined for discharging blood and foul water into the streets, and in 1409 were forbidden from throwing entrails into the streams unless they cut them first into small pieces. And in 1489 if 'any man cast any donge, straw, dede hogge, dogge or catte or any other fylthe into the water wherby the water mought be stoppid' the fine was twelve pence (5p).

# DISHONESTY AND DEATH AT THE HOSPITAL OF ST CROSS

## ENGLAND'S OLDEST ALMSHOUSE?

A mile to the south of Winchester, in the water meadows by the River Itchen, lies the Hospital of St Cross. This is not a hospital in the modern sense, but one of the oldest almshouses in the country. The original founder in the 1130s was Henri de Blois, Bishop of Winchester and brother to King Stephen, who wanted to provide for 'thirteen poor men, feeble and so reduced in strength that they can scarcely, or not at all, support themselves without other aid'. In 1445 another Bishop of Winchester, Cardinal Beaufort, added a second foundation, the Almshouse of Noble Poverty. Today the hospital still accommodates seventeen elderly men known as the Brothers of St Cross, who wear black gowns, and eight Brothers of the Almshouse of Noble Poverty, who wear red gowns. Many writers have been moved by the peace and beauty of the hospital's setting and of its medieval buildings, but things have not always been so quiet and serene.

In nearly 900 years there have been between sixty and seventy masters in charge of St Cross (records vary). Some have been good men but others have diverted the hospital's income to their own use. In the roof of the main entrance archway is a carving of an upside-down face and legend has it that this represents Master de Cloune from the 1370s. He sold off the assets of the hospital, turned out the brothers and began to dismantle the buildings, selling the wood and other materials. He was fined £100 – half to go to the Pope and half to Bishop William of Wykeham's fund for renovating the cathedral – and fled abroad in 1375. The carved face acted as a daily reminder to successive masters not to follow his wicked example.

Probably the most notorious master was Francis North, appointed by his father, the Bishop of Winchester, in 1808. Something of his character can be seen in his response to a petition from the parishioners for a stove to heat the cold, damp church. North replied 'since the parishioners have always done without a stove, they may do without one now'. During his long mastership he helped himself to £250,000 from the funds of St Cross and only resigned in 1861 after a six year fight in the Chancery Court which almost ruined the hospital.

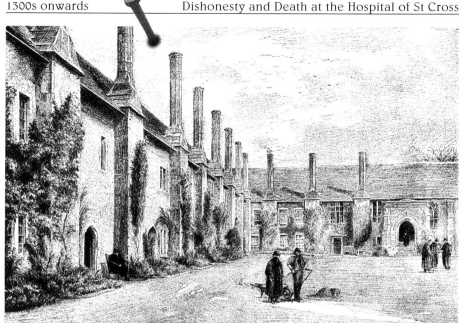

*The Hospital of St Cross, founded in the 1130s, is still an active community today. The 'brothers' live in fifteenth-century buildings, and their medieval chapel is also in use as a parish church. Visitors can claim the 'Wayfarer's Dole', a portion of bread and beer which has been offered free to travellers for nearly 900 years.*

The case is said to have inspired Anthony Trollope to write his novel *The Warden*.

In 900 years there have inevitably also been good and bad brothers living at St Cross – a Richard Cheyne in the time of Master North was said to have been revealed as a mad serial murderer. The misdemeanours of the brothers were usually of a much less spectacular nature. A story which Master Bostock liked to tell in the 1930s was that red brothers were once allowed to bring their servants with them, and that is how one late night a doctor was called to the quarters at the southern end of the range to help in the delivery of a fine bouncing baby.

As in any community, there were rumblings of discontent over the years, echoes of which can be found in the Trustees' minute book. In 1933 the master drew attention to the case of Brother Croft whose wife was giving a good deal of trouble and could not be controlled by her husband. The master was given a free hand to deal with the matter and Mrs Croft was wise enough to accept instruction from him. In the 1940s Brother Radford had to be told he could not call his quarters 'The Rosary' and advertise himself as a rose expert. He had already made 30 guineas and there was some feeling that this money should have gone to the Church. Even the porters were not exempt from bad behaviour, and Thomas Bowsher, the porter in 1899, had to be prohibited from entering any public house in the village of St Cross (of which there were many) having been found intoxicated.

The Hospital of St Cross has been in existence for so many years that graves

*The upside-down face in the roof of the main entrance archway – said to represent Master de Cloune. (Catherine Secker)*

can often be found in unexpected places. In the late 1800s a gravedigger is said to have uncovered the previously unknown burials of twenty people, only four of whom were in wooden coffins, the rest being in rough graves. Burnt floor tiles were found with the bodies, which perhaps lends credence to the story that the Vikings laid waste an earlier church or monastery on the site.

In the late 1800s Brother Lewing recorded in his diary that a dead brother's coffin would be taken into the medieval Brethren's Hall and placed on trestles in the centre. The rest of the brothers came and sat about the catafalque and silently ate a slice of bread and drank a pint of beer. The deceased's relatives were expected to provide a bottle of gin and a cake for the brothers to share after the burial. Bearers were rewarded with a jack of beer. Before leaving the hall the dead brother's badge was removed from his gown, but on one occasion the badge was buried by mistake and the brother's successor was left without a badge until the grave could be re-opened.

Master Humbert in the 1850s revived an old St Cross custom, still followed today, of closing one of the gates of the main entrance under the Beaufort Tower when a brother dies, and leaving the other open. This symbolises that while the gate of earthly life has been closed, the gate to eternal life has at the same time been opened. Another surviving tradition is that the funeral procession stops outside the dead brother's flat. The master asks, 'Brother [name] if you wish to stay then please stay'. As far as we know, no one has ... yet.

## INSANE FROM PAIN

Before the days of modern medicines, and especially painkillers, suicide must have offered a tempting release from suffering. The *Hants Telegraph* for 12 August 1854 reports the inquest on Brother Stephen Lintott, who committed suicide aged sixty-nine. He had been subject to 'excruciating pains caused by a disease to which medical skill could only give temporary relief.' That morning he sent the woman who waited upon him to Winchester to the surgeon of the hospital, and while she was gone hanged himself in one of his apartments with his silk handkerchief. The verdict at his inquest was, 'temporary insanity caused by grievous bodily pain.'

# 1320–1648

# GRUESOME EXECUTIONS

**T**WO OF THE most notorious favourites of King Edward II were Hugh Despenser the elder and the younger. Edward's Queen, Isabella the 'She Wolf', and her lover, Roger Mortimer, captured Hugh the elder at Bristol during their uprising against the king and ordered his execution in the most barbaric way. He was hanged in his armour, cut down and disembowelled alive. His body was left exposed on the gallows for four days before being cut into morsels and fed to the dogs. Hugh had been Earl of Winchester, and so his head was brought here where it was placed on a pole at the top of the castle gate for the purpose of terrifying the citizens.

Hugh Despenser the younger was brutally executed on 24 November 1326 in Hereford. A large crowd gathered in anticipation. They dragged him from his horse, stripped him, and scrawled Biblical verses on his skin. He was then taken to the Market Place and presented to Isabella and Mortimer. He was condemned to hang as a thief, be castrated, and then drawn and quartered as a traitor. The gallows used were 50ft high but he was cut down before he could choke to death. It was

said that just before he died he let out a 'ghastly inhuman howl' much to the delight and merriment of the spectators. After his death his body was cut into four pieces, one of which was sent to Winchester where birds were allowed to peck at the remains.

Edmund Woodstock Plantagenet, 1st Earl of Kent and half-brother of King Edward II, was beheaded outside the castle gate of Winchester in 1340. No local executioner could be found to perform the task and the unfortunate Edmund had to wait on the scaffold for

*The execution at Bristol in 1326 of Hugh Despenser the elder, former Earl of Winchester.* (Froissart's Chronicle)

five hours before one could be found. It was a botched execution with several attempts being made to remove his head.

Executions also took place in the castle itself. In 1603 the Revd Sir George Brooke was executed in the Castle Yard for his part in a plot against King James I. Sir Walter Raleigh was tried in Winchester for his part in the same plot and sentenced to death, but subsequently pardoned. Following a sea raid on the Spanish fifteen years later in 1618 the original sentence was reinstated and he was finally executed in London.

Charles I was held in Carisbrooke Castle in the middle of the Isle of Wight during the Civil War, arriving in November 1647. Captain Burleigh, a man of good family on the island who had been Governor of Pendennis Castle, Falmouth, and who had formerly commanded the king's ship *Antelope*, decided to try to rescue his former master. He was reported as, 'a man of more courage than of prudence or circumspection' and causing a drum to be beaten in the streets of Newport cried, 'For God, the king and the people!' and said he would lead them to the castle and rescue the king from his captivity. This rash attempt was at once crushed by the authorities, even the king's servants urging the people to return home, but poor Captain Burleigh was arrested and tried at Winchester in January 1648 on a charge of High Treason and sentenced to be hanged, drawn and quartered. This sentence was so harsh that no one from Hampshire could be found to perform the task and an executioner had to be brought down from London.

## THE WINCHESTER ORDEAL

Stamford described this ordeal in the middle of the sixteenth century, and in 1648 it was carried out on Captain Burleigh.

That the traytor be drawn from his prison
To the place of execution, as being unworthy
To tread any more upon his mother earth,
Backward, with his head downward, for that
He had been retrograde to dutiful courses:
Hanged by the neck between heaven and earth,
As not deserving the enjoyment of either,
His privities cut off, as having been
Unprofitably begotten, and unfit to leave
Any generation; his bowels burnt, for having
inwardly concealed or concealed treason; his
head cut off, for inventing mischief against
his King and Country; his body quartered and
made a prey for birds, to strike more terror
into others, and to caution them from deserving
the like punishment.

# BLACK DEATH DECIMATES WINCHESTER

**T**HE FIRST OUTBREAK of bubonic plague arrived in England in 1348. In the case of Winchester, it probably arrived through contact with Southampton. It is now estimated that about 50 per cent of the population died and scientists are still arguing as to why it spread so rapidly. In 1348, the only possible explanation could be that God was very angry at the sins of mankind. Bishop Edington of Winchester acted promptly and in October the cathedral priory was ordered to hold additional services on Wednesdays and Sunday. Also, the prior and the monks were to process through the marketplace every Friday, joined by the city clergy and the citizens 'with heads bent down, with feet bare and with fasting' and in silence except for the constant recitation of the Lord's Prayer and the Hail Mary. The procession was to end with Mass in the cathedral. Such gatherings of people could not have been better designed to spread the plague.

The plague was an extremely painful illness to suffer and unpleasant to observe. Classic symptoms were swelling of the lymph gland in the groin or armpits or neck, gangrene on the bodies'

extremities, high fever, muscle cramps and seizures. Death usually occurred within four days.

The cathedral and the citizens almost came to blows over the burial of plague victims. The boundary between the cathedral's land and the area that is now known as The Square was uncertain: near to the cathedral, it had become the city's graveyard but nearer to the High Street, a marketplace. By 1349, there were obviously a large number of burials and space was running out. The Bishop brought a Plea of Trespass against citizens of Winchester for holding markets and fairs and even a tournament on cemetery land which had forcibly obstructed the burial of the dead. On 21 January 1349 Ralph de Staunton, conducting a burial service, had been attacked and the burial disrupted. In June 1349 Winchester citizens, led by the mayor, 'had assaulted, in warlike array and with the din of arms, the bishop's servants and the monks of the cathedral church and men bearing bodies to the graveyard and when these had fled, followed them with noisy threats of burning the cathedral church'. To solve the boundary dispute,

# A PLAGUE ON THE MEDDLING BISHOP OF WINCHESTER!

In the aftermath of the Black Death of 1348, the loss of half the literate workforce presented the Church hierarchy with a major headache. The famous William of Wykeham's solution, as soon as he became Bishop of Winchester (which was then the wealthiest diocese in the land) was to initiate the foundation of places of education. In 1379 he established the 'College St Mary of Winchester in Oxford' (known since 1400 as New College) and endowed 'the College of St Mary of Winchester near Winchester' (now Winchester College) in 1387. This school was originally intended to provide an education for seventy 'poor and needy' scholars keen to progress to a theological education at Oxford.

In 1387 Wykeham ordered 'visitations' to several monasteries. The report was critical of some monasteries and resulted in a personal visitation by the bishop to Selborne Priory. The complete archives of Selborne Priory are an interesting survival now held by Magdalen College, Oxford,

*Bishop William of Wykeham. (Library of Congress, LC-DIG-pg9-01423)*

and give a rare insight into monastic life in the fourteenth century. Following his formal visitation, Bishop William issued a set of thirty-six injunctions implying that lax behaviour and neglect of the rules were running rampant. One twentieth-century scholar who studied the records commented, 'The Prior and Canons, without being guilty of any gross and crying scandal, had become a society of worldly gentlemen living carelessly and very much at their ease.' Wykeham's injunctions included:

* The cloisters were not to be visited by lay people of any sex, and the doors to be kept closed.
* All services should be attended by all canons.
* The rule of silence should be observed.
* Brothers ignorant of the scriptures should be educated.
* Hunting and the keeping of hounds were strictly prohibited.
* The pawning of relics and sacred vessels should cease.
* Buildings should be repaired.
* Canons and brothers should not leave the priory alone, and they should not wear luxurious clothes, or coloured shoes and stockings – the luxurious clothes included garments edged with gold or fur, and girdles of silk, edged with gold and silver.
* Nor should the canons sleep naked without drawers and a shirt!

the king was appealed to and in 1352 a wall was built to delineate the cemetery and that line is still marked by the back of buildings on the cathedral side of The Square. The boundaries between city parishes and the cathedral precinct are still painted on that wall.

The Black Death spared no one; high or low. The prior of the cathedral priory died and the numbers of monks fell from sixty to thirty-five. The priory never recovered its pre-Black Death figures. In 1352, the priory even surrendered its independence to Bishop Edington because of 'need, indigence and misery'. The abbess of St Mary's Abbey also died. Seventeen of the city churches lost their priest and were left to decay. Within the walls, the city shrank. Much of the west and north of the city became wasteland, pasture, orchards and gardens, and were not built on until the 1800s.

This first outbreak of the plague dealt a devastating blow to Winchester, which had not really come to terms with its decline in royal status nor recovered financially from the expulsion of the Jews from England in 1290 (one of Winchester's main streets is still called Jewry Street). The Hampshire downs were sheep country and Winchester, with the River Itchen as its source of energy, had for many years been an important centre of the woollen industry. Following the Black Death the cloth finishing industry, the city's main source of wealth, began its long decline. This was not helped by the removal of the city's monopoly status for selling raw wool in 1353.

Before the Black Death, the population of Winchester could have been as high as 13,000. It did not get back to that figure until at least 1851. The plague

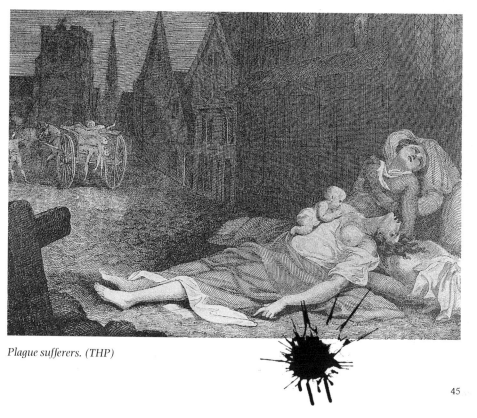

*Plague sufferers. (THP)*

returned ferociously in 1361-62 and children and young men were very badly affected, which reduced the population's ability to recover numerically. This was also the case in 1369.

The plague was to return intermittently to Winchester, with varying levels of severity, for the next 300 years. From the late fifteenth century onwards outbreaks became fewer and more manageable. This was largely due to efforts by the authorities to curtail the disease. It was thought that the plague and all infectious diseases were caused by 'noisome smells' so filth in the streets and streams must be cleared away; they were doing the right things for the wrong reasons.

Winchester's population continued to shrink. In 1440 and 1452 there were two petitions to Henry VI complaining that the decline of the cloth industry within the city had resulted in 11 depopulated streets, 997 empty houses and 17 churches without priests.

It is not always clear from the records in Winchester whether every major outbreak of sickness in the city was bubonic plague. In 1558 there was 'greate sycknes in the Citye'. In 1564 there is an actual reference to the 'plague now remayninge'. In 1593, there was a very serious outbreak and even more extensive regulations were introduced limiting access of people and goods into the city. In September, Anthony Bird, an alderman, magistrate and former Mayor, was accused of going to London to buy curtains which he brought back for his house in Winchester. He had to choose between being locked up in St John's House for fourteen days or having his retail business closed down for a month. From 1603-06, there was plague in the city and suburbs. In 1625, the worst plague outbreak since the Black Death occurred.

The plague returned again in 1665 and in September the Mayor's Feast had to be cancelled; it had been realised by now that large gatherings encouraged the spread of the disease. Winchester College was evacuated to the outlying village of Crawley. The outbreak in 1666 was most severe. To prevent the plague spreading, many victims were shut up in their own houses. The most tragic record is of John Jerome, a cathedral painter and craftsman, who died with his entire family in their home. Plague victims were no longer buried within the city. The area between St Catherine's Hill and Twyford Down, to the south-east of the city, is still known as Plague Pit Valley. Traders would leave food supplies outside the gates and pick up the money for it, left lying in vinegar in the hope of killing any germs.

*Plague Monument. (James King)*

The last recorded plague occurrence was in 1667. These outbreaks created many orphans and the Charitable Society of Natives & Citizens was formed in 1669 to provide education and apprenticeships for them by holding fund-raising dinners. It was joined by the Society of Aliens in 1720. ('Aliens' then meant any resident not born in the city.) The Plague Monument was built in 1758, close to the West Gate and traditionally on one of the sites where the exchange of money and food had taken place, to record the origins of the two organisations.

## THE GREAT REVOLT OF 1381

One of the results of the 1348 plague outbreak was that labour was in short supply in the decades that followed. There was increasing demand for higher wages, lower hours and, from the peasants, freedom from serfdom. The Great or Peasants' Revolt led by Wat Tyler did not just take place in London nor did it just involve peasants.

*Death of Wat Tyler.*

The revolt in Winchester broke out on 17 June and lasted three days. The first day was spent gathering support and threatening those who would not join with death. The Town Bell was rung and the Moot Horn, which can still be seen in the City Museum, was blown to gather people together. Such use implied that the insurgents had some control over the then Guildhall (now Lloyds Bank) in the High Street. On the second day, the insurgents' leader, William Wygge, broke into the King's Staple situated on the street now known as Staple Gardens and, with others, took away documents and burnt them in the High Street. Although Winchester had not been a staple town since 1353, the Staple as a royal court dealing with trade disputes seems to have remained. Walter Hogyn was slain that day: he may have been the guardian of the Staple records. On the third day, Wygge and some of the insurgents went to Romsey to encourage rebellion there.

Unusually, in Winchester many of the rebels were men of standing in the city and their leader was a wealthy draper. They were mainly young men and predominantly from the woollen cloth finishing industry. There appears to have been dissatisfaction with royal (rather than civic) authority over out-of-date and corrupt legal practices, which hampered trade.

The revolt in Winchester was dealt with quickly and severely, probably because the city still had an important image. Within a week four rebels had been executed. Of the twenty-four from Hampshire who were executed or who had fled, fourteen were from Winchester. Surprisingly, Wygge was ultimately pardoned and went on to be five times Mayor of Winchester.

# 1394

# WINCHESTER COLLEGE

**O**N **28 MARCH** 1394 William of Wykeham formally opened his College of St Mary near Winchester with seventy poor scholars, a warden, headmaster and second master, ten priest-fellows, three chaplains, three lay clerks, ten commoners (those who paid for their own food and accommodation) and sixteen quiristers. The scholars were known as

*Engraving of Winchester College. (THP)*

'children', to differentiate them from the commoners. Wykeham's well-known motto was 'Manners makyth man', and his foundation has grown today to be one of the most renowned English fee-paying public schools for boys between the ages of thirteen and eighteen. But over its 600-year history, things have not always been so peaceful and well ordered.

Since a scholarship at Winchester used to give automatic access to New College Oxford, and after that security for life, it is quite remarkable that the early scholars entered Winchester College after only the most superficial of exams. Entrance was more by patronage than by ability and in his statutes Wykeham gave more detailed attention to providing for the chapel and its services than he did to the education of his scholars.

### 'DULCE DOMUM'

Neither the date nor the origin of Winchester's school song 'Domum' are known, but from an extract of an anonymous *History and Antiquities of Winchester* published in 1773: 'according to an old tradition, a scholar was confined to the college during the holidays for some misdemeanor, and denied the enjoyment of relief from study with the rest of the young gentlemen'. One version of this story has him chained to a pillar as his punishment. Apparently this lay so heavily on his mind that after composing the verses of 'Domum' he is said to have pined and died. How true this may be, we cannot tell, but however it came to be written, 'Domum' differs from most school songs in that it dwells exclusively upon the delights of Home. The original song was in Latin, but in English this is how it begins:

> Come, companions, join your voices,
> Hearts with pleasure bounding:
> Sing we the noble lay,
> Sweet song of holiday,
> Joys of home, sweet home, resounding.

In the chorus he seems to find relief by indulging in memories of his happy earlier years:

> Joys of home sing; home, sweet home,
>     sing;
> Joys of home sing; home, sweet home,
>     sing;
> Sweetly, sweetly, sweetly, home sing;
> Joys of home, sweet home, resounding.

His thoughts turn to his mother, and he thinks of the welcome that would have awaited him:

> Roger, ho! 'tis time for starting,
> Haste with horses and traces;
> Seek we the scene of bliss,
> Where a fond mother's kiss
> Longing waits her boy's embraces.

Every year in the distant past, Whitsuntide would be ushered in by a procession of masters, scholars, and quiristers round the pillar to which the poor boy had been chained. They would chant his verses as they walked, keeping alive the mournful tale of 'Dulce Domum'.

## RIOTS AND REBELLIONS

Gentry in the late 1700s were quick to appreciate the learning potential of on-the-job training in the navy, and often sought influential naval captains to take on their sons for a 'gap year' on the high seas. Many of these young men eventually thrived, but then, with the end of the Napoleonic Wars, the Royal Navy began mothballing their warships, and officers and midshipmen alike were laid off or put on half-pay. Youngsters who had dreamed of achieving fame on the quarter deck of a ship of the line were, instead, bundled off by their parents (who had no wish for their elegant country houses to be cluttered up with restless teenagers) to boarding school. So bored did these young men become at school, and so avid were they for adventure, that they rebelled. They even pulled down school buildings and locked their teachers in cupboards.

There were four notable rebellions at Winchester in the late 1700s. The final one in 1793 was a protest against the warden, Bishop Huntingford, and not against the headmaster, Joseph Warton. The warden had decided to punish the whole school for the offence of a small group of boys, who had gone 'out of bounds' to attend a band concert in the Cathedral Close. In response the

*War Cloister (see page 94) designed by Sir Frederick Baker after the First World War and rededicated after the Second World War. (James King)*

boys issued an ultimatum that 'the masters need not trouble to come into School'. They had barricaded themselves into college, and half the paving in Chamber Court had been ripped up for ammunition. The headmaster, coming out from the library, saw the Red Cap of Liberty – a symbol of the French Revolution – fluttering on the Founder's Tower. Warden Huntingford remained in post for another twenty-five years despite this uprising.

To quote A.K. Cook in *About Winchester College*, 'it was in 1818 that, when Alexander Malet hacked at the Warden-bishop's door with an axe, Huntingford put his head out of a window, with the words, "do you know, Sir, that you are assaulting a Peer of the Realm?"' After this pompous outburst, the warden and masters held a parley with the boys from a window, and directed them to write down their grievances. This was done immediately, the list unfortunately starting with 'that you are ugly'. So bad did things become that it took a large number of infantrymen with fixed bayonets to quell the riot. Two open revolts in twenty-five years seems more than a coincidence, but it should be remembered that revolution was not unusual at the time.

## 'NOTIONS'

It might not be surprising to find remains of an ancient dialect in some remote place untouched by modern communications, but it is very strange that words which have been dead in the English language for centuries should have survived in the traditions of a school. Winchester College has retained its own vocabulary, known as 'Notions'; the second edition of the *Winchester Word-Book* published in 1901 is a sixty-five-page dictionary of all the words then in use in the school vocabulary. In the introduction we are told '*in those days, at Winchester they would never* send *a person, but would* fierk *him: they were never* idle *but they* thoke plentifully: *a thing was not* pretty *but* cud: *when* dead-brum [broke] *they would get some* bulky pax [rich friend] *to pledge* them dibs [lend them money]: *they used to* mug [study] *at* toy-time [homework] *on* remedies [half-holidays]: *they would* splice rocks [throw stones]: *they got* planted [hit by a football] *and* killed [hurt badly], *and it* worked [hurt] dreadfully ...' Fewer of these traditions and words survive as the years go by, but Winchester still uses some language that goes back many centuries.

# LEGITIMISING THE TUDORS

## THE LEGEND OF KING ARTHUR – TUDOR DIPLOMATIC 'SPIN'?

Henry Tudor defeated Richard III – the last monarch of the royal house of York – at the Battle of Bosworth Field in 1485, and thus ended the Wars of the Roses which had occupied much of the late 1400s. On the battlefield Lord Stanley picked Richard's crown from a bush where it had fallen and placed it on Henry's head, and this was the last time in English history that the royal succession was determined in battle. Henry successfully restored stability to the monarchy in England and founded the Tudor dynasty. After a reign of nearly twenty-four years, he was to be succeeded by his son, Henry VIII.

In 1485 Henry VII married Elizabeth of York, the beautiful daughter of Edward IV, thus uniting the Houses of Lancaster and York. In 1486 Prince Arthur was born in Winchester; he was baptised in the Lady Chapel in Winchester Cathedral to create a symbolic link with the legend of King Arthur and Camelot. It seems that Queen Elizabeth thought that the beautiful black Tournai marble font, given to the cathedral by Bishop Henri de Blois 250 years earlier, was too exposed for the occasion, and ordered that a smaller silver font should be brought specially from Canterbury for the baptism. Arthur's brother Henry was born five years later in 1491.

Since Henry was the younger son and was not expected to become king, we have relatively little information about his early life. At the age of ten he was certainly involved in the wedding celebrations for his elder brother Arthur and Katharine of Aragon in November 1501, but Arthur died at the age of fifteen in 1502, after less than five months of marriage. Their mother also died when Henry was only eleven.

The young Henry immediately became the natural successor to the throne, and he shouldered the burden of his older brother's duties, succeeding to the throne in 1509 aged eighteen as King Henry VIII, and promptly married his brother's widow Katharine. Following the mismanagement of the country during the final years of his father's reign, Henry VIII had the challenge of restoring confidence in

## KING ARTHUR

The legend of King Arthur dates from the end of that period in English history which is often known as the 'Dark Ages' – between the departure of the Romans after AD 400 and the arrival of the Saxons some 200 years later. There is no written history covering this period, so matters of importance would have been passed down from parent to child by word of mouth; probably the bedtime stories told to children to get them to sleep. There is evidence that there was a strong tribal leader who may have been called Arthur, and he is likely to have had a following of knights who he may have encouraged to maintain a strict moral code. How much of the alleged 'magic' associated with the story has any base in fact is another question, but the legend of Arthur crops up in several places - Tintagel, Glastonbury, Snowdonia, Cumbria and Winchester, as well as in Brittany.

Eight hundred years later, in 1485, Sir Thomas Mallory published *Morte d'Arthur* in which he places Camelot at Winchester. This book is in reality a collation of stories collected from the original legends, and put together in such a way that they appear to be real history rather than a work of fiction.

the monarchy, and England's position in Europe – which still gave allegiance to the Pope in Rome as head of the Christian Church. Henry VIII visited Winchester in 1522 when he invited Charles V – the most powerful ruler in Europe at that time – to a banquet in the Great Hall of Winchester Castle. Charles had been crowned Holy Roman Emperor in 1519 by Pope Leo X, and ruled over the Hapsburg Empire and the newly unified kingdom of Spain. Henry had been given the title 'Defender of the Faith' by Pope Leo in 1521, so these were two of the three most influential monarchs in Europe – the third being Francis I of France who was antagonistic towards the other two, who between them controlled far larger territories.

The Round Table in the Great Hall of Winchester Castle is one of the great treasures of the city. According to legend, it is the table around which King Arthur and his Knights of the Round Table met, and it has been famous for centuries for its associations with the legendary 'Once and Future King'.

Originally the table stood on the floor with twelve outer legs and a central support. It measures over 18ft in diameter, weighs nearly 1¼ tons and is constructed from English oak. It is too large to get in or out through any of the doors, so must have been put together in the hall, where it has hung as an ornament since probably the fifteenth century.

Its timbers have been dated using tree-ring and radiocarbon techniques to around 1280. It was probably created for a tournament near Winchester to celebrate the betrothal of one of Edward I's daughters. The first record of its painting is in the early years of Henry VIII's reign. In the centre is a Tudor Rose – a combination of the white

*Winchester's Round Table in the Great Hall of Winchester Castle. (James King)*

and red roses of York and Lancaster. It is believed that the portrait of a king on his throne labelled 'King Arthur' is actually a portrait of a young Henry. Around the circumference of the table in ancient script are the names of Arthur's twenty-four Knights of the Round Table.

On the occasion of Charles V's visit, Henry VIII entertained him in the Great Hall where the Round Table on the wall was intended to give the impression that Henry could trace his ancestry back to the reign of King Arthur. A similar story is told at Hampton Court Palace where there is a large painting of St George slaying a dragon, and guess whose face St George has – Henry VIII's! Henry was of course only the second monarch of the House of Tudor, who were Welsh, so this looks a lot like Tudor 'one-upmanship'.

# 1534–40

# END OF AN ERA

## DISSOLUTION OF THE MONASTERIES

The Dissolution of the Monasteries by Henry VIII in the 1530s dealt Winchester a severe blow from which it took many centuries to recover. The city had three great Benedictine foundations whose origins went back to Anglo-Saxon times – the cathedral priory, the nunnery at St Mary's and Hyde Abbey. In addition there were the more recent friaries, famed for their work with the urban poor. These religious houses not only supported a sizeable population of monks, nuns and priests, but were also an important source of employment for lay people and provided the medieval equivalent of our modern Social Services and NHS – support to the poor and sick. Within a decade of Henry VIII declaring himself the Head of the English Church in 1534, all such ancient institutions had been closed.

In 1536 Henry VIII's Commissioners visited St Mary's Abbey and found twenty-six nuns, all living virtuous lives, but in addition over seventy lay sisters, schoolchildren, servants and officers connected with the abbey.

The buildings were 'of great and large compass, environed around with many poor households which have their only living of the said monastery'. The nuns also ran a sistern hospital to care for sick members together with poor and sick relatives. St Mary's was closed in 1539 and the remaining nuns pensioned off. Only one wished to move elsewhere – a reflection of the difficulty for women to find a new vocation – and in 1540 the abbess and several nuns still seem to have been living together in the old abbess' lodging. In their wills they touchingly left bequests to each other. Twelve poor sisters were allowed to remain in the

*Stone coffins from St Mary's Abbey, uncovered by archaeologists in the 1970s, can be seen in Abbey Passage to the east of the Guildhall. (Clare Dixon)*

*Abbey House, one of several fine town houses built on former monastic land after the Dissolution. (Clare Dixon)*

hospital but, without the nunnery, this could only be a temporary arrangement. The building was eventually divided into tenements before being used as a prison.

The great abbey church itself and its immediate buildings were declared 'superfluous'. The plate and other valuable items went to the king and lead from the roof – and even from between the stained glass of the windows – was used at his new castle at Hurst on the Solent. Archaeological excavations have revealed two empty graves in the nave of the abbey church, and we can imagine a distressing picture of relatives removing the remains of their loved ones before the desecration of the church.

In 1554 the abbey site was given to the Corporation of Winchester to help defray the wedding costs of Mary Tudor. The ruins were further dismantled and sold, cartloads of stone being bought by Winchester College in 1566 and used to repair its boundary wall (where it can still be seen today). The eastern part of the site was used in the late seventeenth century for a substantial town house with extensive gardens, appropriately

called Abbey House and in use today as the official residence of the Mayor of Winchester. The western part was eventually cleared of tenements and industrial uses in the nineteenth century for the construction of the Victorian Guildhall.

Meanwhile, at the cathedral priory, the shrine of St Swithun was dismantled on 21 September 1538 at the unlikely hour of 3 a.m., presumably to avoid any trouble. The three Commissioners reported to Thomas Cromwell: 'Pleaseth your lordship to be advised that this Saturday, in the morning, about three of the clock, we made an end of the shrine here at Winchester. There was in it no piece of gold, nor any ring, or true stone, but all great counterfeits. Nevertheless we think the silver alone thereof will amount to two thousand marks ... we intend to sweep away all the rotten bones that be called relics.' And thus the bones of St Swithun, a focus for pilgrims at the cathedral for many hundreds of years,

## BUTCHERED BY THE DEVIL

There was said to be an ancient curse on anyone who seized the manor of Godbegot in the centre of Winchester from the monks of the cathedral priory – they would be placed in the devil's own cauldron and the butchers of hell would carve their flesh for ever. A very appropriate curse, as the real-life butchers of Winchester had their flesh shambles in that area. Perhaps that is why the Dean and Chapter ended up as owners and not the king!

were lost for ever. A legend says that the monks hid the bones away before the King's Commissioners came, but if so it was in too safe a place – they have never been found.

The next year, the priory (monastery) at the cathedral was closed, although the cathedral itself was kept as a place of worship run by a new Dean and Chapter. It's tempting to see a clever bit of footwork in the appointment of the last prior of the monastery, William Basing, as the first dean with a pension of nearly £200. Other members of the new Chapter were also former monks – but with much more modest pensions. The priory had been a rich and well-endowed institution, and all of Winchester felt the loss of its spending power and the employment it generated.

The entire appearance of Winchester had been changed by the Dissolution.

In place of the great religious houses there were some fine town houses, including one built by Richard Bethell on the site of Hyde Abbey, Abbey House on the site of St Mary's, and Eastgate House opposite it on land formerly occupied by a Dominican friary. But Speed's map of 1611 also shows empty areas within the city walls, with most of the population living in the suburbs.

A new pattern of social support also had to emerge. Poor relief and health care became lay responsibilities, while prosperous citizens reacted to the plight of the sick and elderly by founding almshouses. The transformation from the old ways to the new is neatly mirrored in the use of 100 loads of stone from the ruins of Hyde Abbey to help build Christes Hospital, an almshouse founded in 1586 by Peter Symonds, stepson of Richard Bethell.

## THE 'WINNERS'

Thomas Wriothesley (pronounced Risley) was one of Henry VIII's courtiers who did very well out of the Dissolution of the monasteries in Hampshire. He acquired over a fifth of the monastic manors in the county, became Earl of Southampton and later Lord Chancellor. Appropriately, his fine new house was created out of the shell of Titchfield Abbey.

Winchester College not only gained some fine stone to repair its walls, but also land belonging to the former friaries within and outside the walled city.

The City Corporation almost doubled its number of properties within the city walls. Offsetting this new land and income, however, were new responsibilities for relief of the poor and sick.

# 1554

# AN UNHAPPY MATCH

## MARY TUDOR AND PHILIP OF SPAIN

One of the last great royal ceremonies to be held in Winchester was the marriage in 1554 of Queen Mary Tudor to Philip, heir to the kingdom of Spain. The marriage was a turning point in English history, but in the end brought little joy either to the royal couple or to the country.

Mary's father, King Henry VIII, had made himself Head of the Church in England in 1534, breaking the link with Rome. Protestantism had spread under her brother, Edward VI, but his death in 1553 brought Mary to the throne. Mary was a Catholic and determined to restore the authority of the Pope over the English Church.

What Mary needed to secure England as a Roman Catholic country

*Mary and Philip had exchanged portraits, but only met each other two days before the marriage. (THP)*

was a husband and, urgently, an heir. At thirty-seven, she must have known that time was running out.

The man chosen was Philip of Spain, to whose father, the Emperor Charles V, Mary had been betrothed as a child. Philip was only twenty-seven years old and, according to the Spanish ambassador, 'so admirable, so virtuous, prudent and modest as to appear too wonderful to be human'. Be that as it may, the match was not popular in England where any attachment amongst the ordinary people to the 'old religion' did not extend to welcoming a foreigner into the government of the country. Encouraged by the French, there was much plotting amongst discontented English nobles, and Sir Thomas Wyatt marched on London with a band of Kentish rebels. However, Mary retained the upper hand, a number of plotters were executed (including the teenage Lady Jane Grey) and the marriage plans went ahead.

Why were the royal couple married in Winchester and not in London? It was near the port of Southampton, where the Spanish party could land, and as a smaller and more conservative city than London, there was less likely to be public opposition. From a symbolic point of view, Winchester had connections with the Tudor dynasty and especially with Mary's uncle, Prince Arthur, Katharine of Aragon's first husband. Finally, the Bishop of Winchester was Stephen Gardiner, Lord Chancellor and a loyal Catholic, who had been freed from the Tower by Mary on her accession and so was an ideal person to conduct the wedding.

For Winchester, the honour was a doubtful one. It was not at this time a large or wealthy city, and the practical difficulties of staging a royal wedding at short notice were considerable. The ceremony was planned for 25 July 1554 (feast day of St James, patron saint of Spain) but preparations were slow, and as late as 14 June a letter was sent to the Privy Council 'touching the want of things at Winchester, praying them to consider the same and to return an answer with diligence'. It was not until 15 July that twelve carts laden with treasury were sent from the Tower of London to help meet the expenses. These were many and varied, from 5s for painting the arms of the Lord Chancellor on the West Gate, to 13s 4d for Queen Mary's trumpeters, and 4d for a proclamation against those who spoke ill of the king and queen. The rubbish was cleared away from the city streets, the High Cross or Buttercross in the High Street was mended for 19s, and the vast sum of £6 18s 10d was allowed for the provision of wine.

Other things were harder to arrange, even with the necessary funds. The cathedral had suffered damage during the reformation and hurried steps had to be taken to cover this up and to restore some of the colour and beauty which would once have been provided by painted statues and highly decorated side altars. On the day, a contemporary account reports that the cathedral was 'richly hanged with arras and cloth of gold'. The marriage itself took place on a small platform, covered with a rich carpet of silk and gold, which had been constructed at the entrance to the choir. Cathedral visitors can still see the chair, covered with purple velvet secured with gilt-headed nails, on which it is said that

Mary sat. The hooks on the nave pillars from which tapestries were hung are still occasionally used today for brightly coloured banners.

Mary was staying with the Bishop of Winchester at Wolvesey Palace, and the couple did not meet until Philip arrived from Southampton two days before the marriage. He may have had a nasty surprise. Not only was Mary a decade older than Philip, the Venetian ambassador described her as unattractive, wrinkled, very short-sighted and with a voice rough and loud like a man's. However, as a contemporary noted, 'The king understands that this marriage was effected not for the flesh but for the restoration of this realm'. Philip seems to have made a considerable effort to make himself pleasant to the English, even to the point of drinking tepid English beer, but not everyone was pleased with Winchester. Its 100 inns and alehouses were surely appreciated by the English guests, but the Spaniards complained of being over-charged, cramped ('only the early comers get good lodgings'), having no employment (Philip was served by the English household which Mary had given him) and even of being robbed on the roads. They thought the ladies of the court 'not beautiful' although 'many in number'.

The wedding was followed by a great feast and ball at Wolvesey Palace, and a few days later Philip and Mary left for Basing House near Basingstoke on their way to London. How different

*The East Hall of Wolvesey Palace where the celebrations were held for Mary and Philip's wedding. (James King)*

English history might have been if their union had resulted in an heir. Despite the Bishop of Winchester blessing their marriage bed, Mary's pregnancy turned out to be false and Philip left England after just over a year. He returned in 1557 to find Mary ill and left again for the final time a few months later, having persuaded the English to join his war against France. The disappointing result was the loss in 1558 of Calais, England's last French possession, and grief is said to have hastened Mary's death later that year. She was succeeded by her half-sister, Elizabeth, against whom, thirty years later, Philip would launch the Spanish Armada. One bright spot, from Winchester's point of view, was that Queen Mary granted rents from former monastic properties to the Corporation in recognition of the expenses of her wedding – and as a result its income doubled!

# 1547–1603

# TORTURE, IMPRISONMENT AND DEATH IN THE NAME OF RELIGION

**T**HE 1500S WERE a time of swift religious change. Henry VIII seized authority over the Church in England from the Pope in 1534, and Protestantism spread under his son, Edward VI. Queen Mary restored Catholicism, but then under Queen Elizabeth England became once more (and has remained) a Protestant country. Any opposition to the official religion was taken as opposition to the monarch and many people, of all social ranks, found themselves facing imprisonment or death for having the 'wrong' Christian convictions.

The Bishop of Winchester in 1534 was Stephen Gardiner, an international politician who used his legal expertise to help King Henry VIII annul his marriage with Anne of Cleves and arrange the marriage to Catherine Howard. Gardiner fought against what he saw as the extremes of Protestantism and was imprisoned in the Tower under Edward VI, only to be released and reappointed Bishop of Winchester by Queen Mary. One of the highlights of his career was to conduct the marriage of Mary to Philip of Spain in Winchester Cathedral. An elaborate chantry chapel was prepared in the

cathedral for his burial, which is now used as a chapel for Christian unity.

John White, his successor, had been warden of Winchester College and was sent to the Tower under Edward VI as a prominent Catholic. Queen Mary freed him and made him Bishop of Winchester in 1556. However, giving an oration at Mary's funeral, he said that 'the dead are

*Bishop Stephen Gardiner, who as Lord Chancellor was responsible for condemning a number of Protestants to death under Queen Mary.*

more praised than the living', which was taken as an insult to Queen Elizabeth and he was again imprisoned in the Tower. He lost the bishopric and was later buried secretly in Winchester Cathedral, contrary to Elizabeth's wishes. He was not given a memorial and his remains were only found in 1886.

Another victim was John Philpot, Archdeacon of Winchester. He had been appointed during Edward's reign but on Mary's accession was brought before the Bishop of London for refusing to give up his Protestant faith. He has left a record of 'the second night of my imprisonment in his [the Bishop's] coalhouse where I, with my six companions, housed together in straw as cheerfully as others in their beds of down.' He was sent to Newgate Prison, where as many irons were put on his legs as he could bear, and was afterwards burned at the stake in Smithfield.

Only one person was burned at the stake in Winchester. Thomas Benbridge came to the attention of the authorities in 1558 for his religious beliefs, probably verging on Puritanism. He was questioned many times by John White, Bishop of Winchester, but refused to recant. On being led to the stake he began to prepare for his ordeal with seemingly great courage and even alacrity, undressing himself, and disposing of his clothes to the persons present. However, when feeling the heat of the fire on his legs, Benbridge cried out, 'I recant.' His friends rushed forward to withdraw the lit faggots and the sheriff stopped the execution. Benbridge was made to sign his retraction on the spot but, back in prison, changed his mind and so a fortnight later was returned to the stake for a second time.

Queen Elizabeth famously declared that she had no wish to 'make windows into men's souls' and for most of her reign Roman Catholics in Winchester lived in relative peace, assuming they could afford to pay the fines for non-attendance at the established church. Lady West's house (on the site of what is now the Royal Hotel in St Peter Street) was searched in 1583, revealing a hidden chest with mass vestments, chalice, communion bread, Mass books and catechisms. There was also a portable altar in the Ladies Chamber, but there is no record of Lady West suffering any punishment. However, with the growing fear of plots centred on the imprisoned Mary Queen of Scots, and with Philip II of Spain's enmity, persecution was stepped up and Catholics were increasingly seen as traitors.

*A rather idealised portrayal of a burning.*

Two local schoolmasters, John Slade and John Body, were arrested in 1583 for refusing to take the oath of the queen's supremacy over the Church. John Body had been to Winchester College and seems to have kept a school between Winchester and Andover. They were tried together at Winchester and again in Andover and condemned to death in both places. John Slade was drawn on a hurdle, hanged, disembowelled and quartered in Winchester and John Body suffered the same fate in Andover.

In 1591, Roger Dickonson, a Catholic priest, was caught for practising in the neighbourhood of Winchester. Also arrested for helping him was Ralph Milner. Dickonson was sent to London, where he was tortured, and both were condemned and executed in Winchester. The judge offered Milner his life if he would attend the established church, even once, but he refused. At the place of execution in Winchester, his seven children were brought to him in the hope that the sight of them might get him to recant. It didn't work. He gave them his blessing and declared that he could wish them no greater happiness than to die in the same cause.

Seven single ladies from Winchester and its surrounding area, whose houses John Dickonson had visited to administer the rites of the Roman Catholic Church, were also tried. The judge thought to terrify them by condemning them to death but, on the contrary, they were filled with joy and afterwards burst into tears when he gave them a reprieve.

James Bird became a convert to the Catholic faith and went abroad for a Catholic education. On his return, he was arrested, tried and condemned for having made himself a Catholic. His liberty was offered to him, as it had been to Ralph Milner, if he would only once attend a Protestant service. His father, Anthony, who fell foul of the plague regulations in the same year [see page 46], begged him to accept, but he answered, 'he always would be obedient to his commands, except where they interfered with his duty to God.' After a long imprisonment, in 1593 aged nineteen, he too was hanged, disembowelled and quartered. His head was set on a pole over one of Winchester's gates.

# 1642–1651

# A ROYAL PAIN: ANOTHER CIVIL WAR

I N 1642 THE ongoing power struggle between the Monarchy and Parliament broke out into civil war. A large proportion of the population of Winchester were Royalists supporting Charles I, but the castle was owned by Sir William Waller, a staunch Parliamentarian, so when war was declared it was hardly surprising that the city should see conflict.

The Civil War started quietly: on 10 August 1642 two gentlemen from Wiltshire were robbed of £80 by a small band of straggling Royalists near Hursley village. The culprits were caught drinking at Romsey, taken to Winchester Castle and there imprisoned. The next recorded event was far more serious: Parliamentarian and Royalist forces clashed near Wherwell, some 10 miles from Winchester on 12 December 1642. During the skirmish the Royalists cut off a band of Parliamentary forces and captured their colours. Pursued by overwhelming Parliamentarian forces under Sir William Waller, the Royalists retreated to Winchester and closed the city gates.

When Waller arrived at the north gate he immediately ordered the city to be surrounded, stopping any provisions

entering and preventing any Royalists from escaping.

The Parliamentarians stormed the city's west wall, where the ancient structure had been partially broken down, but the ditch was still extremely steep. The Royalists retreated into the castle, which was immediately besieged. The citizens of Winchester paid £1,000 to the Parliamentarian forces to spare them and the city from pillage, but despite this the city and especially the cathedral close were ransacked, with Parliamentarian troops stealing everything they could find. During this attack on the city the Royalists lost between thirty and forty men, whilst the Parliamentarians only lost three or four.

The next day Waller threatened to fire the castle gate. The trapped Royalists sought a parley and agreed to surrender the castle, their arms, horses and money, hoping to receive quarter. When they opened the castle gate they were immediately assaulted and their possessions stolen, with even their clothes torn from their backs.

The next day the Parliamentarians turned their attention to the cathedral, as an eyewitness describes:

On Thursday morning the 14, between nine and ten of the clock, the doors of the cathedral were violently broken open and the army prepared to deface that glorious church. They (the Parliamentarians) did enter the church with their colours flying, their drums a beating and their matches fired. Some rode their horses up the aisle of God's house. On reaching the altar they did rudely pluck down the table and broke the rail which they did later burn. They burnt the books of common prayer and all of the singing books. They tore down the organ, the monuments to the dead they defaced, and some they near demolished. They did break all of the window glass. The mortuary chests carrying the bones of the ancient kings were brought down and the bones scattered. They broke open the muniment house and plundered all of the church plate and ancient charters.

Afterwards they did ride around Winchester wearing surplices with such hoods and tippets, much to the disgust of the townspeople of Winchester.

Waller's troops left Winchester laden with loot. The city was reoccupied for a short time by Royalist forces but by March 1643 Waller had retaken the city and for the second time it was pillaged:

The muniment house again was broke into, ledgers and register books, charters and deeds, writings and muniments lost, divers of them thrown into the river, some picked up by the brethren of St. Cross. Divers large parchments they did make into kites and flew them in the air.

*Graffiti in Winchester Cathedral dated 1642, probably carved by a Roundhead soldier of the Civil War. (Don Bryan, reproduced by kind permission of Winchester Cathedral)*

Waller left the castle with a small garrison, but Lord Ogle retook it in the name of the king, immediately strengthened it and built outer works at Oram's Arbour and on St Giles's Hill.

In March 1644, Lord Ogle was summoned to a Royalist council of war in Lord Hopton's lodgings at Eastgate House. Despite Ogle's objections, it was agreed to take on Waller's army, and the next day Lord Hopton marched out of the city with his army whilst Ogle remained to hold the castle. The subsequent Battle of Cheriton on 20 March, although not decisive, was nevertheless to prove a turning point in the war, with the Royalists on the defensive from that time onwards.

After the decisive Parliamentarian victory at Naseby on 14 June 1645 the 'business of Winchester Castle was now to be seriously undertaken'. The House of Commons passed several Bills to supply men, artillery, ammunition and provisions to destroy the castle at Winchester.

'On the Lords day the 28th September 1645 at eight of the clock, Lieutenant-

## TORTURED FOR HORSES

Master Say was the son of a cathedral canon, who had entrusted the concealment of his horses to his servant. However, some of his neighbours betrayed him and Master Say was brought before Waller who questioned him about the horses, and handed him over to the Provost Marshal with orders to make him confess:

This official conducted him to the George Inn between the High Street and St George's Street (now the site of Barclays Bank), and led him into what was long known as the 18 stall stable. Placing a halter round his neck, the Marshal renewed his cross-examination. Obtaining no information, he hoisted him up to the rack, allowing him to hang until he was almost strangled, and then gave him a little breathing space, this process was repeated several times, until the spectators of this barbarous scene quitted the stable in disgust. Finding torture ineffectual, the Marshal with many kicks and blows dismissed Master Say, who for a few days afterwards was reported as dangerously ill, a circumstance scarcely to be wondered at.

General Oliver Cromwell came before Winchester with 7000 men and set down outside the city'. Cromwell had several large cannon and mortars, along with demolition experts. He was opposed by Lord Ogle and a mere 700 men inside the castle, although they were well armed and provisioned. Formal letters were exchanged between Ogle and Cromwell with Ogle refusing to surrender. On Saturday 4 October the guns opened fire and continued to bombard the castle into Sunday. Then sappers exploded charges under the castle wall, causing a breach some 30ft wide.

At the pleading of his garrison Ogle sought a parley. This was immediately accepted and Articles of Surrender were drawn up, stating that the Royalists were to leave the castle with all its weapons in place; Ogle's men could take their horses and personal possessions with a guarantee that they would not be despoiled of their goods.

The agreed departure time for the withdrawal from the castle was delayed because 'the Governor and some of the Officers, being unwilling to leave any wine behind them, had made themselves very drunk – and Lord Ogle was as drunk as a beggar and had to be helped on to his horse'.

In 1649, the Council for State, concerned that Winchester Castle should never again pose a threat, resolved that its defences should be dismantled. The county was at first reluctant but finally agreed in 1651. Under the supervision of Richard Major of Hursley Park, whose daughter had married Cromwell's son, many of the walls were thrown down and the castle destroyed. The Great Hall, although badly damaged, survived and is the only remaining part of the original castle above ground today.

# 1685

# DEATH TO DAME ALICE LISLE!

The trial of Dame Alice Lisle on a charge of treason was the first in what has since been known as the Bloody Assizes and was held in Winchester on 25 August 1685. It took place after an unsuccessful rebellion, led by the Duke of Monmouth – an illegitimate son of Charles II, and a Protestant. The purpose of the rebellion had been to seize the throne from Charles's brother King James II – a declared Catholic. Dame Alice was the only victim condemned in Winchester, though in the subsequent circuit of trials of Monmouth's supporters, overseen that month by Judge Jeffreys in Salisbury, Dorchester, Taunton and Wells, more than 1,000 were either condemned to death or were transported to the West Indies. What was the background to this landmark trial, the story of which is portrayed to this day in a mural in the Houses of Parliament?

Alice Beconshaw was the second wife of Sir John Lisle, a prominent lawyer and politician who was elected MP for Winchester in 1640 and served in the Long Parliament. Lisle was also Master of the Hospital of St Cross on the southern edge of Winchester for five years from 1644. He was one of Cromwell's trusted supporters and served on the tribunal which condemned King Charles I to death, though he did not sign the death warrant, and he had sworn Cromwell into Office as Lord Protector.

Following the Restoration in 1660, to avoid trial in England for regicide, Sir John fled to Switzerland where he was assassinated in 1664. His widow, Dame Alice, returned to Hampshire. Following involvement in a plot in 1683 to assassinate both Charles II and his younger brother James, Monmouth exiled himself to Holland and gathered supporters in The Hague, still hoping to accede peaceably to the English throne. The accession of James on Charles's death in February 1685 put an end to these hopes; James was intent on restoring Catholicism and absolute monarchy in England.

In May 1685 Monmouth put together a small force and sailed from Holland in three ships landing at Lyme Regis – staunch Protestant territory – hoping to attract further support for his cause on arrival. After two months Monmouth's

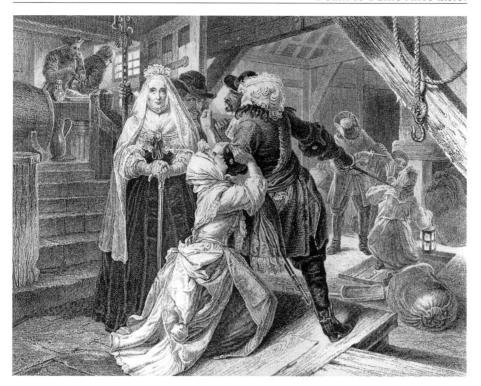

*Alice Lisle sheltering the fugitives, from a mural in the Houses of Parliament. (THP)*

campaign in Dorset and Somerset ended at the Battle of Sedgemoor on 6 July 1685. Monmouth fled, but was captured on the western side of the New Forest, and subsequently executed on Tower Hill.

Dame Alice Lisle meanwhile continued to live at her family home, Moyles Court at Ellingham in the New Forest. It is quite likely that she visited her son and his family at Dibden Manor House also in the New Forest – one of the places her ghost is still said to walk!

Following the Battle of Sedgemoor in 1685, two fugitives from the battle sought refuge at Moyles Court. These were John Hicks, a dissenting preacher, and Richard Neglethorpe, a lawyer. The men spent the night at Moyles Court, and were arrested the following

morning. Initially Dame Alice had denied their presence, but they were soon found, and she was charged with harbouring traitors.

At her trial Dame Alice employed no counsel and simply stated that she had given the two men shelter, completely unaware of their involvement with Monmouth; although she knew who Hicks was, she had simply accepted Neglethorpe as his friend, and didn't know his name.

She pointed out that her husband had been a staunch follower of Cromwell, that her son had actually fought against Monmouth, and that it was therefore most improbable that she would risk the ruin of her family and indeed risk her own life by harbouring traitors.

Odious as the law was, it was strained to the limit for the purpose of destroying Alice Lisle ... The witnesses prevaricated. The jury, consisting of the principal gentlemen of Hampshire, shrank from the thought of sending one of their own class to the stake for conduct which seemed deserving of praise rather than of blame. Jeffreys was beside himself with fury ... He stormed, cursed, and swore in language which no well-bred man would have used at a race or cock-fight ...

The jury retired, and remained long in consultation. The judge grew impatient. He could not conceive, he said, how in so plain a case, they should even have left the box. He sent a messenger to tell them that, if they did not instantly return, he would adjourn the court and lock them up all night. Thus put to the torture, they came, but came to say that they doubted whether the charge had been made out. Jeffreys expostulated with them vehemently, and, after another consultation, they gave a reluctant verdict of Guilty.

*Macaulay*

It has been suggested by Lord Macaulay, the Victorian historian, that if Lady Alice knew her visitors had been involved in the rebellion then she was certainly technically guilty of treason, but could equally be praised for committing an act of mercy. He goes on to suggest that no English ruler except King James II has had the barbarity even to think of putting a lady to such a cruel and shameful death for so trivial a transgression.

Jeffreys' treatment of her in court has been particularly condemned – although his biographer states that there is some doubt about the reliability of the only account of the trial. Following sentence, at the intercession of the Clergy of Winchester, a respite of five days was granted. Judge Jeffreys recommended her to the king for a pardon; as his biographer says: 'it was James who pointedly denied mercy on this', though he allowed beheading, as befitted her station, to be substituted for burning at the stake.

Dame Alice was beheaded on 2 September 1685 outside what is now the Eclipse Inn, in The Square at Winchester, where a wall plaque records the event. The execution provoked national outrage. Apart from Lady Lisle's advanced age – she was seventy years old at the time – and saintly reputation, her husband had been a noted Parliamentarian, yet she had hidden supporters of a Royalist pretender. James II's vicious severity after Sedgemoor was undoubtedly a significant factor in his enforced abdication in 1688 in favour of Prince William of Orange.

It is reported that the tall grey shade of Alice Lisle now haunts the area where she spent her last night on earth – the Eclipse Inn. This is one of four locations reportedly haunted by her, along with Moyles Court, her former home, and Ellingham Lane where a driverless coach and horses has been seen. It has also been claimed that her ghost haunts the site of her son's home, Dibden Manor, carrying her head under her arm.

# 1738–1867

# HANGINGS, BURNINGS AND POOR FANNY ADAMS

**W**INCHESTER WAS ONE of the principal courts in the land, and many significant trials have been held in the Great Hall; execution was a gruesome public spectacle until well into the nineteenth century.

In December 1776 James Aitken, a British sympathiser for the American colonies in the War of Independence, tried to burn down Portsmouth Dockyard – one of the first ever terrorist acts on British soil. He has gone down in history as Jack the Painter. A petty criminal, Aitken had gone to each of the Royal Dockyards in England, and had also developed an incendiary fuse.

In December 1776 he set a fuse in the Dockyard Rope-house. After trouble lighting his fuse he rushed out, and made his escape, looking back and seeing flames.

Hundreds of men fought the blaze, including marines, yard workers and sailors. There was little damage, but near panic resulted. Newspapers across the country reported the fire; even the king followed developments. The authorities were soon on the trail of Aitken, who had previously been spotted lurking around the Dockyard.

He was finally arrested for housebreaking at Odiham in North Hampshire, charged with the Dockyard fire, tried for High Treason and convicted and hanged in March 1777. His trial at Winchester was a huge public event, and dominated newspapers and magazines. Even his execution was a spectacle, as he was hanged from the mizzen mast of the frigate HMS *Arethusa*. After death his body was hanged in irons at Fort Blockhouse at Gosport, across the Harbour entrance from Portsmouth.

*A nineteenth-century public hanging. (THP)*

69

Between 1735 and 1819 Winchester's public executions took place at Gallows Hill, near the Jolly Farmer pub in Andover Road. There is a small display in the pub about some of the victims of the nearby gallows. It is thought that perhaps 230 felons were executed here. Most were men but women were also hanged, though if women had committed murder they were often burnt at the stake, also at Gallows Hill.

One was sixteen-year-old Mary Groke or Grote, convicted of Petty Treason for poisoning her mistress, Justine Turner. On Saturday, 18 March 1738 Mary was tied to a hurdle and drawn along behind a cart carrying two other felons. On arrival at Gallows Hill Mary had to wait as the two men were hanged before she was led to a large wooden stake. She was then chained to the stake and bundles of faggots were placed around her. The executioner would next have strangled her with a noose to make her unconscious before lighting the fire.

Gallows Hill was popular with the residents of Winchester who loved a good hanging, and came in their thousands to watch the females burnt to death. The burning of Mary Bayley in 1794, and the last execution of this kind in Winchester, that of Mrs Huntingford in 1819, were watched by so many people that the magistrates decided all future executions should take place within the precincts of the County Gaol in Jewry Street instead of on Gallows Hill.

Meanwhile, the County Gaol in Jewry Street was redeveloped on the site of the original thirteenth-century one at a cost of £10,000 and was criticised for being 'too opulent for prisoners'. Between 1821 and 1849 a total of eleven felons were executed here, with a gallows erected on the roof so members of the public could watch from outside the prison. In 1849 another new prison was completed in Romsey Road. Executions continued to be carried out on the roof of the prison, many thousands of spectators watching from Romsey Road as the victims were led to the gallows. Such was the scene on 24 December 1867 when estimates put the number of spectators at nearly 5,000, mostly women. They had come to watch the public execution of Frederick Baker.

In August 1867 a young girl, Fanny Adams, and her friend Minnie, both eight years old, were playing with Fanny's seven-year-old sister Lizzie. They were close to their home in Alton and Fanny's mother had no worries about their safety. The girls were approached by a respectably dressed man, who had been drinking and was later identified as Frederick Baker. He offered Lizzie and her friend a halfpenny to go off and he also offered Fanny a halfpenny to go with him up a nearby lane. Fanny refused to go so he picked her up and carried her off.

The two girls returned home without Fanny and told neighbours what had happened. One neighbour went in search and met the same man coming down. She asked him what he had done with Fanny and he said he had met her but had left her safe and well earlier in the afternoon. He said he was a respectable clerk to a local solicitor, so he was allowed to pass. When Fanny had still not come home for supper, a search party set off to look for her. They found poor Fanny's dreadfully mutilated remains in a hop field so the police went to interview Baker.

They found bloodstains on his clothing and a knife. He was arrested and his trial, held at Winchester Assizes, started on 5 December. On 20 December the jury found him guilty of the murder of poor Fanny Adams, who was buried in Alton cemetery where her grave can be seen today.

About the same time, the Royal Navy introduced tins of mutton as a more reliable way of preserving meat on ships. The sailors complained that there was very little meat in the tins, and gloomily declared that the butchered contents must surely be 'Sweet Fanny Adams'. This term rapidly became abbreviated to 'Sweet FA', a term which has come to mean 'little or nothing'.

Frederick Baker's execution was the last public one to take place in Winchester. Because of the crowds and the chaos they caused, the authorities decided that all future executions would take place inside the prison away from public view.

*Fanny Adams' grave in Alton Cemetery.*
*(James King)*

## 1680s ONWARDS

# SICKNESS AND SOLDIERS IN THE KING'S HOUSE

**W**ITH WINCHESTER'S PROXIMITY to Channel ports, it was always likely to have the military based here en route to fight the many wars Britain got involved in. Thanks to Charles II dying too early, the army was eventually garrisoned in a Wren-designed palace instead of being billeted on the reluctant population. The king had been a great enthusiast of horse racing and so thoroughly enjoyed the racing near Winchester that the King's House, an English 'Versailles' built on the site of Winchester Castle, was started in 1682. The building was nearly finished when Charles II died in 1685. Subsequent monarchs were not able or interested enough to finish it: Winchester had a large and prominent white elephant in its midst. The first occupants were troops but not British ones. From 1756, whilst the Seven Years War was raging, the King's House was used for up to 5,000 prisoners of war, mainly French. During the American War of Independence, in 1779 a French hospital ship was captured and its sick occupants were brought to the King's House, bringing their 'malignant pestilence' with them. In the

overcrowded and insanitary conditions, large numbers of prisoners died, as did many gaolers. The prisoners were buried in the former castle ditches.

As the French Revolution developed into the Reign of Terror, aristocrats and clergy fled the country. Permission was given by George III, in 1792, for the King's House to become a refuge for about 1,000 French, mostly clergymen. However, as Britain became involved in the Revolutionary Wars in 1793, it was decided that the King's House should be made into barracks. So from 1796, 2-3,000 troops were 'more commodiously lodged, than perhaps in any other barracks in the Kingdom'.

The King's Royal Rifle Corps, associated with Winchester since 1794, was permanently based in the King's House from 1855 and joined in 1858 by the Rifle Brigade. Other regiments continued to pass through Winchester. In 1855 the *Hampshire Chronicle* reported that six soldiers from one of these regiments were charged 'with a violent assault and threatening conduct towards Wm. Luckett, landlord of the Three Hearts, a beer house of very low repute, situate on the Lawn ... and with malicious damage,

*The King's House in use as barracks. (W. Savage c. 1880, Winchester City Council Museums)*

done on the premises.' Following a quarrel with the landlord the night before, the soldiers had returned with the intention of murdering him. Luckett managed to escape but his pub was wrecked.

Other buildings were added to the Upper Barracks such as the hospital alongside Romsey Road, guard rooms on the Romsey Road entrance and the Officers' Mess on St James Lane side of the site. The Lower Barracks were developed and this included a chapel, with a school room adjoining and a prison. There was great controversy when the chapel was being converted into a cinema in 1995 as to whether the crosses should remain on the roof (they did).

The local volunteer militia, under the overall command of the Lord-Lieutenant of the county, had been created to defend their part of the country should it be invaded. They were 'embodied' in Hampshire for the first time in 1757 during the Seven Years War and the North Hants Militia were based in Winchester. Serles House in Southgate Street, now the Royal Hampshire Regimental Museum, became their unofficial headquarters. In peacetime, the local militia would be 'disembodied' but in Hampshire, until 1828, they had to meet annually in Winchester for a month's training. In his diary Lieutenant Colonel Peter Hawker, the militia's second-in-command, in 1825 writes:

Our training in Winchester ... is this day at an end! And so should I have been also, had I been obliged to weather another such month, what with sitting to midnight over sloe-juice [sloe-gin], occasional suppers etc (kept up till morning), plays, balls, grand singing dinners, and in short one incessant round of company ... The little duty which I had to do was the only mental recreation which this sink of dissipation would afford.

Winchester no longer has a palace designed by Wren. In 1894, fire broke out in the King's House. The city fire engines were situated in the Guildhall, at the other end of town, and soldiers were sent down to haul the fire engines up, to save time in harnessing the horses. However, there was a problem in getting a sufficient water supply. The palace could not be saved and so all the fire-fighting effort was directed onto the Great Hall. The first plan to replace the King's House was for nine lines of hut-style buildings, but fortunately for Winchester the chief army surveyor got involved and designed four new elegant buildings in Wren's style.

Apart from the two world wars, dealt with elsewhere in this book, the barracks remained the permanent depot for regiments that, despite many changes of name and organisation, always had a link with the original King's Royal Rifle Corps of 1755. Even now the current amalgamated regiment has been called The Rifles since 2007. In 1964, the barracks were re-furbished and renamed Peninsula Barracks in honour of The Rifles' involvement in the Peninsular War (1808-1814) under the overall command of Wellington. The Hampshire Regiment, nicknamed the Tigers after their regimental mascot

---

One of the North Hants Militia, Thomas Thetcher, lies buried in the Cathedral graveyard. On his gravestone is written that he:

died of a
violent Fever contracted by drinking
Small Beer when hot on the 12th May
1764, Aged 26 years

It is the oldest surviving named monument to an ordinary British soldier. An American soldier, Bill Wilson, whilst visiting the city towards the end of the First World War, noticed Thomas Thetcher's headstone and the reason for his death. As an alcoholic later in life, the wording on the tombstone came back to him and was one of the inspirations behind his co-founding of Alcoholics Anonymous in 1935.

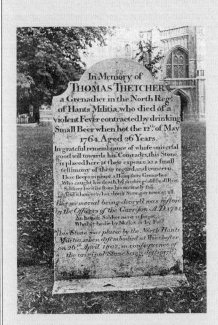

*Thomas Thetcher's gravestone. (Library of Congress, LC-D420-3306)*

and entitled Royal in 1946, was based in Winchester from 1877, ultimately in the Lower Barracks. In 1992, they merged with the Queen's Regiment to become the Princess of Wales Royal Regiment and are the senior infantry line regiment of the British Army.

After the Second World War, conscription remained in operation until 1960, with the last National Service soldier leaving the army in 1963, so Winchester remained a lively military place. Uniformed men on the streets were a common sight. Various pubs became recognised as drinking places for different ranks: officers would be found in the Wykeham Arms or Southgate Hotel (now the Hotel du Vin), senior NCOs used the South Western near the railway station (now the Registrar's Office), corporals and upwards would drink in the West Gate, with their riflemen using the Bakers Arms or the Green Man. Alcohol-fuelled fights were frequent occurrences in the city; the passageway beside the Bakers Arms off the High Street was known as Blood Alley. In the past, recruits were known to frequent Canon Street, the red-light district of Winchester, though now a highly respectable area.

By the late twentieth century, the military was no longer such an influence on life in Winchester. Peninsula Barracks, on the site of the castle and the King's House, was closed in 1985. Some buildings were retained by the Ministry of Defence as museums and

## THE GREAT DUKE OF WELLINGTON

### From Waterloo to Winchester – 1815–1852

Wellington, the Great Hero of Waterloo in 1815, was given the estate of Stratfield Saye in northern Hampshire in 1817 by a grateful nation. He was made Lord-Lieutenant of the county in 1820 and thus began a long association with Winchester, the county town, until his death in 1852. He paid a three-day visit to Winchester shortly after his appointment where he was treated like royalty. He was made a Freeman of the City in the old Guildhall in the High Street, there was a dinner and ball in his honour in St John's Rooms on the Broadway and visits were made to the cathedral and Winchester College, with cheering crowds wherever he went. There was, however, an undercurrent of protest. Wellington was a member of an unpopular Tory government who was introducing very repressive measures against any social unrest. 'Several of the gentlemen were insulted and man-handled' as they entered St John's Rooms for the dinner.

By the time Wellington was eighty-three and visiting Winchester in August 1852, for what would be the last time, he was regarded as a 'national treasure'. Completely gone was his earlier unpopularity. He was seen as a fair-minded elder statesman who had given Britain and Europe over thirty years of peace. Wellington died in September and the nation was plunged into deep mourning. Winchester, like other cities, marked the day of his funeral in London by the cathedral bell tolling all day and shops shutting at lunchtime as a mark of respect.

offices, but the rest were eventually sold to a developer who planned to demolish most of it, including some of the Wren-style buildings, to be replaced by modern housing. One Winchester architect, Huw Thomas, managed to persuade the developer to keep most of the buildings and convert them into residences. So a whiff of Versailles has been preserved for the city, enhanced by the formal gardens on the former parade ground.

Peninsula Barracks closed with an emotional evening parade of 'Beating Retreat' which ended with a lone bugler sounding the ''Last Post' from above the pediment of one of the buildings. Sir John Moore Barracks on the northern edge of the city became the Army's new barracks, now home to the Army Training Regiment, and troops make less impact on the city. However, regiments historically associated with Winchester still march through the city on their return from active service overseas and the citizens turn out to welcome them.

# 899–1999

# MORE WANDERING BONES

**W**E HAVE ALREADY told the story of Alfred's life and his connections with Winchester, where he died and was buried. But what happened to his bones after that? It's a simple question with an answer involving at least two exhumations and complicated enough to take up a whole chapter.

The first part of the story is clear enough. King Alfred was buried in the Old Minster, predecessor of today's cathedral, in 899. However, tradition says his spirit was unquiet and haunted the Minster until his bones and those of his wife, Ælswitha, were moved to the newly constructed New Minster next door. Here, in due course, their son, King Edward the Elder, was also buried.

By Norman times, the New Minster's site in the centre of Winchester, between the enlarged Royal Palace and the new Norman cathedral, was becoming too cramped. In 1110 it moved to an area called Hyde just outside the North Gate, where a new abbey church and monastery were constructed. We can imagine the monks leaving the New Minster for Hyde in a rather grisly procession, carrying with them the bones of Alfred, Ælswitha and Edward along with relics such as the skull of St Valentine, bones of St Barnabas and a great gold cross donated by King Canute and Queen Emma.

The bones of Alfred, his wife and son, were reburied in front of the High Altar in the new abbey church. Here they lay undisturbed until the Dissolution of the Monasteries when, in 1538,

*An artist's impression of King Alfred produced during the twentieth-century Hyde Abbey archaeological excavations. (Winchester City Council Museums)*

Hyde Abbey was surrendered to the king. John Leland, an antiquary who travelled around the country at this time, reports that:

> The bones of Alfredus, king of the West-Saxons, and of Edward his sunne and king, were translatid from Newanminstre, and layid in a tumbe before the high altare at Hyde: in the which tumbe was a late founde 2. litle tables of leade inscribid with theyr names. And here lay also the bones of S. Grimbald and Judoce.

Itinerary of John Leyland 1535 – 1543

Bridewell became a common term for a prison, but the name comes from a London residence of King Henry VIII, Bridewell Palace. This in turn took its name from a nearby holy well dedicated to St Bride. The palace became a prison in the 1550s.

The bridewell at Hyde, started in 1788, was for less serious offenders with 'only half corrupt minds'. One of the few remnants of its buildings today is a marker stone dated 1788 on the south-east corner of the site.

The abbey church was demolished within a year of the Dissolution, and if such lead tablets were indeed found, they have since been lost. Part of the site was developed for a Tudor mansion house, but the rest was still covered in rubble in the late eighteenth century when it was bought for the construction of a bridewell.

One of the first tasks of the Bridewell prisoners was to clear away the rubble, which they seem to have done by digging pits to bury the larger pieces of masonry. According to Captain Henry Howard, an antiquarian who questioned the prison warden a few years later, the site of the High Altar and the three royal graves was found during this process in an area being prepared for the governor's garden. There had been a coffin made of a single block of stone 'cased with lead both within and without' containing some bones, and two other coffins. However, the prisoners had thrown the bones about, the lead was sold, the coffin broken and the fragments then reburied in a deeper pit 'for the sake of the garden'. Howard certainly believed the great coffin to have been Alfred's, and the other two coffins those of his wife and son.

Next on the scene was yet another antiquarian, John Mellor, who carried out more excavations in 1866 after the demolition of the bridewell. Even at the time there was some scepticism over his claim to have discovered Alfred's tomb intact, but he exhibited the bones he had found as Alfred's in the county hospital at Winchester and in London. They were eventually reburied in a grave outside the east end of St Bartholomew's, the parish church of Hyde, where a ceremony is still held every year on the anniversary of Alfred's death. However, the grave is marked only with a cross, reflecting the doubt over whether it really is Alfred buried there.

An attempt was made to answer some of these questions with an archaeological 'dig' led by Winchester Museums Service in the summers of

*Hyde Abbey Garden was designed to reflect the features of the east end of the abbey church, discovered during excavations in the 1990s. The three stone slabs mark the former positions of the three royal graves. (Clare Dixon)*

1997-99. The east end of the abbey church was identified during the excavation, and also the site of the High Altar. A large early pit, probably that dug by the bridewell prisoners, was found in the right position to have contained the royal tombs. However, the twentieth-century archaeologists found it empty apart from some masonry fragments and one late medieval human bone. If the royal coffins were once there, they are no longer.

In 2013 the bones from St Bartholomew's have again been exhumed and are being tested scientifically. This may shed some light on the puzzle, but it is possible we will never know for certain where Alfred's bones are today. However, three stones set within Hyde Abbey Community Garden mark the place where it is believed he and his family lay for more than 400 years – in front of the High Altar of Hyde Abbey.

# 1817

# WHAT KILLED JANE AUSTEN?

**O**N THE FACE of it, Jane Austen cannot be regarded as one of Winchester's medical success stories. In May 1817, she travelled from her north-east Hampshire home in Chawton to lodgings in 8 College Street so she could be attended more conveniently by a doctor in Winchester, only to be dead by July. Also, bearing in mind she spent thirty-six of her forty-one years in Hampshire, there is only solid evidence that she ever visited the city twice, the second time being when she came to die. However, Winchester does have her bones, buried in the cathedral; seemingly at her request.

It is unfair to cast a slur on Winchester just because Jane Austen died here; she even makes a reference to the 'capital surgeons' of Winchester. It was one of them, Mr Giles King Lyford, from a distinguished family of Hampshire doctors already known to the Austens, and who was Surgeon-in-Ordinary to the Parchment Street hospital, who attended her at Chawton and recommended she come to Winchester.

Jane Austen, from the gentry class, would never have been a patient at the hospital, which was for the 'Poor Sick'.

In fact her family contributed to the cost of running the hospital; her father the Revd George Austen, subscribed a guinea in 1765, only to withdraw his subscription later that year. Her brother Edward, the inheritor of the Chawton estate, contributed five guineas in 1805.

Jane Austen did have one happier stay in Winchester. In 1814 she and

*Jane Austen based on a sketch by Cassandra, 1810. (Library of Congress, LC-USZ62-103529)*

her beloved elder sister Cassandra came on 26 December to stay for a few days with a childhood friend Mrs Elizabeth Heathcote. She was the widow of a canon living in what is now 11, The Close. Jane may have visited Winchester on other occasions: Cassandra, in a letter after Jane's death, refers to the cathedral as 'the long low building that she [Jane] loved' which hints at greater familiarity than might have been gained by her short visit in 1814. During Jane's final stay she was only able to get out of their lodgings in College Street once, and then in a sedan chair.

Jane seemed to be in reasonable health in her first few weeks in Winchester, but in June Mr Lyford warned the family to expect the worst. She was well enough to dictate a humorous poem to Cassandra on 15 July three days before she died; about it having rained on St Swithun's Day because the Winchester races had taken place on that day without asking the saint's permission.

Medical historians are still divided as to what she died of but it is highly probable that, whatever it was, it would not have been curable then. Without a scientific examination of her bones, they can only go on the symptoms that Jane and others mention in their letters. In a letter in 1817 Jane herself refers to being 'black & white & every wrong colour'. In 1964 her symptoms were diagnosed as Addison's Disease, a disease of the adrenal glands, treatable now but unrecognised then. Later Hodgkin's Disease was suggested, as was a form of cancer and also tuberculosis. However, her symptoms are not consistent with any of these diagnoses. One recent researcher has even suggested that the

*No. 8 College Street - Jane and Cassandra's rooms were on the first floor. (Winchester Tourism)*

basis for Jane's ill health was her being in her mother's womb for ten months. George Austen wrote to his sister-in-law about the delayed arrival of Jane, his seventh child, in December 1775 and joked that he and his wife had 'in old age become such bad reckoners.'

Jane Austen died at 4.30 on the morning of 18 July 1817, with Cassandra by her side. Her body was placed in a coffin on the ground floor of No. 8 until the funeral on 24 July. It was to be no celebrity event. On the day of the funeral, the coffin was closed and placed on a low bier with a pall over it and wheeled along College Street and into the Cathedral Close. It was accompanied by three of Jane's brothers, Edward, Henry and Francis and her nephew James Edward Austen. From the doorway of No. 8, Cassandra watched 'the little mournful procession the length of the Street'. The burial service in the north aisle of the cathedral had to be over before the usual Morning Service took place.

Having the death on his hands of someone who was to become recognised as one of England's greatest novelists does not seem to have done Mr Giles

King Lyford any harm. He resigned from the hospital in 1819 having by then become 'Extraordinary & Consulting Surgeon', with his son Henry appointed to take his place. He also resigned at the same time as Surgeon of the City Gaol in Jewry Street and of the Bridewell in the suburbs of Hyde. After this he was to become Mayor of Winchester, in 1824, 1829 and 1833. On his death in 1837 aged seventy-three, the *Hampshire Chronicle* records that, 'he was one of the most distinguished provincial surgeons of this county'.

## WINCHESTER AT THE FOREFRONT OF MEDICAL FACILITIES IN THE EIGHTEENTH CENTURY

Winchester was the first place outside London to have a hospital since the closing of monastic hospitals following the reformation in the 1500s. In 1736, Dr Alured Clarke, a canon of Winchester Cathedral, founded a hospital supported by private subscription in the south-west corner of Colebrook Street in an existing medieval building (demolished in 1959 and now the site of Colebrook Street Car Park). The ethos of the new county hospital was one of treating the 'Poor Sick' with much care and tenderness, as well as providing medical care in a clean environment. Rules for staff and patients were equally strict. Nurses could be dismissed for treating patients badly and there was certainly one case where a nurse was dismissed for hitting a patient. Patients had to be recommended by sponsors who would be prepared to pay for any necessary funeral expenses and could also not be suffering from a terminal illness on entry. They could not leave the hospital without permission, they had to attend prayers regularly, men and women could not visit the others' wards without permission, no cards, dice or any other games were permitted and, amazingly for the times, no smoking was allowed. If patients were fit enough to do some work they could, but only around the hospital such as helping with other patients, cleaning and ironing. From very early on, it was recognised that the sixty-bed hospital was not big enough and very often the number of out-patients tested the hospital finances. So in 1753 the hospital was moved to Clobury House, a very grand-looking seventeenth-century house in Parchment Street which was now to be enlarged and adapted for use by the hospital.

By this time Winchester was attracting doctors because of the excellent reputation of those already there, such as the Lyfords. The provision of a hospital in Winchester was just one aspect of the city's recovery from centuries-long decline, since it had lost its position as one of the nation's principal cities. Winchester was beginning, by the mid-1700s, to provide the services that one would expect from the county town that it is today. The church, college, Assize Court and hospital created a core of professional people who required the services of many different trades and shops. A short social season during the winter months developed, with some of the gentry building large houses in the city centre, of which many remain. St John's House, with its grand assembly room created within a medieval building in 1769, was the scene of many a ball, dinner and concert.

# 1800s

# DISEASE, DRAINS AND DIARRHOEA

## MUCKABITES V ANTI-MUCKABITES, 1800S

A feature of medieval Winchester was the open streams or brooks which ran through the lower part of the city. The city authorities made regulations and imposed fines in an attempt to keep them clean, stating for example in 1554 that the brooks were to be stopped yearly to be 'scallied, scowred and lett go within ten days.' Failure to do this cleaning could result in imprisonment. By the middle of the nineteenth century, however, with a growing population putting increasing strain on traditional methods of waste disposal, the brooks were shockingly full of filth and spreading disease.

As late as August 1866 the *Hampshire Chronicle* was still posing the question:

> Did the citizens of Winchester consider that the vast outlay which would be required for the carrying out of the sewerage of the city could be profitably expended, considering the means at disposal and the probable greater healthfulness of the locality.

To our modern way of thinking, the answer is self-evident. Of course a growing city, with a population of about 15,000, needed a sewerage system. To those on Winchester's City Council in the mid-1800s, there seemed to be arguments on both sides. Opinion hardened into two camps, nicknamed the Muckabites (against the installation of mains sewerage) and the anti-Muckabites (for).

The anti-Muckabites could see that cesspits had become inadequate to deal with the quantity of waste being produced, and that disease was resulting. Their camp included many (but not all) medical men, together with those involved in the running of Winchester College, the cathedral and the barracks. These last three institutions all had an interest in keeping down disease but also, very importantly, were exempt from paying local taxes.

The Muckabites, who for many years maintained their majority on the City Council, included shopkeepers and small businessmen who didn't want to see taxes rise to pay the considerable capital costs of installing mains drainage. Many such members of the respectable

## THE
# MUCKABITE'S
## TRIUMPH.

*Air.—"The STRAND."*

Good health to all the Muckabites,
        Heigh ho! *Stink* O!
Who love to have their Dirty Nights,
        Heigh ho! *Stink* O!
Our Cesspools shall not be Drained,
        Heigh ho! *Stink* O!
Our Slush-holes shall be retained,
        Heigh ho! *Stink* O!
As for Fevers, we dont fear,
        Heigh ho! *Stink* O!
So long as we can get strong Beer,
        Heigh ho! *Stink* O!
Nor yet for Cholera do we care,
        Heigh ho! *Stink* O!
If Death does come and at us stare,
        Heigh ho! *Stink* O!
So it's good-bye all ye Sewerites,
        Heigh ho! *Stink* O!
We mean to die firm Muckabites,
        Heigh ho! *Stink* O!

*'The Muckabites Triumph'. The anti-sewerage party feeling confident. (Winchester City Council Museums)*

classes had in any case moved out of the centre of town into new villas in the suburbs or on West Hill, well away from the problem. The people who were suffering were the poorer classes in the lower parts of the city such as The Brooks area, many of whom were living in overcrowded tenements as the urban population grew.

The picture we have of central Winchester at this time is shocking. The only way to get rid of sewage was into cesspits, but the high water table and drainage from higher parts of the city meant that these often leaked into wells, cellars and under floorboards. These very wells were a major source of drinking water, whilst children collecting drinking water from the river with buckets had to wade into the centre to avoid floating sewage. More filthy liquid waste was being produced by the slaughterhouses, while many poor families still kept a pig in their yard. The formation of the Winchester Water Works Co. by local entrepreneur Charles Benny, only added to the problem. Many new suburban houses were connected to piped water, as were buildings on the western hill such as the barracks, workhouse and what is now the University of Winchester. But still the waste water could only drain away downhill into streams, the river or already-overflowing cesspits and wells. Not surprisingly, the death rate in The Brooks and other low-lying areas of Winchester was 30 per cent higher than on West Hill. An outbreak of cholera in 1848 killed thiry-four people, all in the lower part of the city.

The main hospital in Parchment Street, central Winchester, both suffered from and contributed to the drainage problem. In 1861 the governors employed a civil engineer, Robert Rawlinson, whose report 'The sanitary conditions of the Hants County Hospital' was damning. 'The City of Winchester ought to be sewered ... it is only a question of time ... as to when a devastating epidemic shall prevail,' he thundered. He noted that the hospital site was undrained, the sub-soil wet, the size of the cesspool only adequate to deal with surface drainage, and the result was that the soil was continually saturated. Overflow was draining into the open stream of Upper Brook Street. He could only recommend moving the hospital to a new site. Amongst those supporting this opinion was Florence Nightingale, whose father was on the hospital committee.

An important feature of the new drainage scheme was the pumping station in Garnier Road. This is surely the only sewage pump in the country to be associated with a cathedral dean – Dean Garnier, a champion of the poor and unemployed and influential anti-Muckabite, who died in 1873 aged ninety-seven. The pumping station was opened in 1878 and still stands, although its two beam engines are gone. Another surviving relic of the long battle over mains drainage may be the Filth Drain. A council workman in the 1950s claimed to have explored a brick-lined tunnel running downhill through the city. Perhaps it is still there, like the three brooks which run – clean now but in culverts – under the roads of lower Winchester.

*Garnier Road pumping station, c. 1900. At one time household refuse was used as fuel, being cheaper than coal, but the prominent chimney has now been demolished. (Winchester City Council Museums)*

In 1868 the hospital did indeed move to a new site on West Hill, opposite the prison (which had moved out of the city centre in the 1840s). The new building still had no mains drainage and, while conditions on the hill were more sanitary for its patients, the situation in the city centre was hardly improved. A 'Filth Drain' continued to carry overflow from the cesspools of the hospital and prison into the brooks at the bottom of town. Even after the city eventually introduced sewers, the hospital did not benefit as it was outside the city boundary. The hospital architect, Butterfield, had done his best to design a system of drainage, but it was not properly maintained and in 1877 outbreaks of fever began to be noticed amongst patients. Twenty years later, in 1897, the hospital was finally joined to the city's sewerage system.

Meanwhile, the 1860s saw the anti-Muckabites collecting information to support their case. A committee was formed to visit houses in the lower city and reported on places where windows could not be opened because of the stench from privies, on privies opening directly onto the open streams, on wells filled with sewage and on the contamination of the well serving the town pump. The average life expectancy in Winchester was found to be fifty-eight, but in the parish of St Peter's Chesil, by the river, it was only forty-two. Finally, forced into action by national legislation, Winchester adopted a sewerage scheme in 1877 – thirty years after the first committee had reported in 1849 that a system of mains drainage for the city was a matter of the first importance!

# 1906–1911

# WILLIAM WALKER
# MVO – 'DIVER BILL'

**W**INCHESTER CATHEDRAL USUALLY sits just above the natural water table – the crypt often floods in the winter. In January 1905 the cathedral architect submitted a regular report on the building to the Dean and Chapter. His main concern was the state of the south wall of the retrochoir. This area at the east end of the building had been added in the thirteenth century, and the cathedral appeared to have broken its back at the point where the retrochoir joined the original Norman building. The Dean and Chapter acted immediately, and sought further advice from a specialist architect, Mr T.G. Jackson. He had an exploratory trench dug, and found that the thirteenth-century builders had formed their structure on a timber raft to spread the load of the walls, unaware that not far below their raft was a thick layer of waterlogged peat. Over time this compressed under the load of the new building. Below this peat was a bed of hard gravel which would make an excellent foundation, but which lay nearly 6m below the water table. What the medieval builders had failed to appreciate was that they were building over the original course of one of the

streams of the River Itchen, diverted 1,000 years earlier by the Romans. Initial attempts to remove the peat resulted in flooded holes as water pressure burst through the last few inches of peat from below. Mr Jackson realised that he needed a civil engineer, and he engaged Francis Fox, a descendant of a former Bishop of Winchester, Richard Fox, and a member of the London firm Douglas Fox and Partners. Fox's proposal was that damaged areas should be stabilised, and then underpinned down to the hard gravel.

Work started on the underpinning of the cathedral foundations in 1905, but the water level was causing very slow progress and it was not until April 1906 that Fox had a brainwave. Why not use a diver? This would remove the need for constant pumping, which had been causing erosion of the solid material beneath the walls. William Walker was one of two divers engaged initially, but it was soon realised that he could do a better job on his own, with the assistance of a team of normal construction workers on the surface.

The method used was to dig a 'drift' from outside about 4ft wide and at

*The pub named after the diver who saved Winchester Cathedral from collapse 1906-1911. (James King)*

William Robert Walker was born on 21 October 1869 in Walworth, London. He had four brothers and a sister. William left school at sixteen and joined the Royal Navy where he trained in Portsmouth as a deep-sea diver. He left the navy aged twenty-five and joined the firm of Siebe Gorman, famous for the manufacture of diving equipment. His first wife, Hannah Cashmen, gave him five children, but died in 1900, within a year of the birth of the youngest when William was only thirty-one, and working for Siebe Gorman extending Gibraltar Dockyard. William sent the children home, asking his widow's family to look after them. Within a year he had married Hannah's younger sister Alice; they had a further six children.

right angles to the wall. Digging down to the bottom of the stonework it was possible to remove the original 700-year-old beech tree trunks forming the raft, which were found to be in good condition. Workmen then dug the drift right under the walls, as much as 20ft in, and dug down to the peat and part way through it, leaving about 1½ft of peat. The loose spoil was removed, and then Walker removed the remaining peat, so that the hole filled to the top with water flooding up through the gravel. Working in a black peat 'soup' under water, he then lined the bottom of each hole with a layer of bags full of dry cement which set under water sealing the bottom of the drift, and then moved on to the next drift. Once the cement had set, water could be pumped out, and solid foundations could be built by normal

*Another sculpture of William Walker, near the Cathedral Refectory. (Reproduced by kind permission of Winchester Cathedral)*

my pipe? Don't lay it down there.' Just sticking out from the drift there might be a stone coffin, and he say, 'This is one solid mass of germs down there.' I laughed and said, 'No, I keep them in my pocket for you.'

When work was completed, a great service of celebration was held in the cathedral. This was attended by King George V who, as a royal naval cadet, had been taught to dive by Walker, who was subsequently appointed MVO – the personal gift of the king – for his work on the cathedral. In 1918 an epidemic of Spanish flu swept across Europe and William contracted the disease which developed into acute pneumonia. He died four days later on 30 October 1918 aged forty-nine and is buried in Beckenham, Kent.

bricklayers using concrete blocks and hard engineering bricks. William worked on the foundations for over five years with few breaks, and virtually the whole cathedral was underpinned.

It was thought that there might be some danger of infection as the diver was working in a graveyard, but his remedy for any possible ills was tobacco. As soon as he reached the surface the first thing he did was to light his pipe. His assistant was a man called William West, who stayed in Winchester after the contract was completed in 1911, and was still alive when the BBC made a programme on St Swithun's Day 1956 to mark the fiftieth anniversary of the start of work in 1906. In his BBC interview, West said:

I think Bill's habits were like mine. He was fond of a smoke, and when he come up for a spell sometime, somebody told him about germs, which didn't worry him. And he say, 'Where's

For over fifty years there was no memorial in the cathedral to recognise the contribution of William Walker in saving this great building. In the 1960s it was decided to commission one, but it seems that the brief given to Sir Charles Wheeler, the chosen sculptor, gave him an incomplete picture of what was expected. The cathedral archive contains many fascinating details of the statue project, which refute the frequently told story that Wheeler was given a photo of the wrong man.

In due course Wheeler created a charming sculpture of a generic diver, but it was not a likeness of Walker, and his family were deeply disappointed. It took another forty years before the original statue was replaced with one which is a true likeness of Walker; this was unveiled in 2005, and now stands in the retrochoir.

# 1770–1908

# A FEW MORE RIOTS!

## THE BUTTERCROSS RIOT – 1770

Cranbury Park at Otterbourne is an attractive private estate shielded from public view, about 5 miles south of the centre of Winchester. In the 1700s the estate was bought by the Dummer family. Meanwhile the Paving Commissioners had decided that Winchester's beautiful early 1400s High Cross or Buttercross, which stands in the High Street, was in some way obstructing street development. So in 1770 Thomas Dummer arranged to buy it intending to erect it as a feature in Cranbury Park. Unfortunately no one had consulted the residents of Winchester.

Thinking that the deal was agreed, Mr Dummer sent his workmen with their wagons and horses, and the tools to dismantle the structure, but they were met with a crowd of outraged citizens who 'organised a small riot' and drove them off; the workmen returned to Cranbury with their wagons empty. Discovering that he could not have the original cross, Mr Dummer cancelled the deal and had a lath and plaster copy made for his park, which stood there for

about sixty years until wind and rain finally demolished it. Meanwhile, the original Buttercross was heavily restored by Sir George Gilbert Scott in 1865, and still stands in its original position in the High Street at the western end of the Pentice. Of the four large figures on the

*Winchester's High Cross or Buttercross, only saved for Winchester by a 'small riot'.*

cross, three are relatively new but the oldest statue, facing the nearby building and sheltered by it, is probably of St John the Evangelist.

## THE SWING RIOTS – 1830

The period after the Napoleonic War was a time of unrest in Britain. Population growth and troops returning from the wars fuelled unemployment, a situation made worse by the increased use of machinery on the land. The end of the war also meant more competition for farmers as the continent was now free to trade grain with Britain. The impact of the French Revolution was still very fresh in the minds of the land-owning classes.

Unrest began in Kent in July 1830 and spread to Hampshire in November where trouble was widespread throughout the county, lasting for just over a week. It manifested itself in various ways – the breaking of threshing machines; incendiary attacks on ricks and barns; public meetings to get wage increases; demands for money from farmers, and also for lower rents and more generous Poor Law allowance.

Isolated protest was not revolution but this trouble was spreading so quickly and seemed so widespread with the name 'Captain Swing' cropping up so frequently, could this be revolution? They became known as the 'Swing Riots' since threatening letters sent to many prominent residents in the countryside

At ten o'clock, the five Special Commissioners entered accompanied by the High Sheriff, followed by the Lord-Lieutenant – the Duke of Wellington of Waterloo fame.

Over the next ten days, the Commission dealt with nearly 300 cases. On 29 December, Henry Cook who had struck a glancing blow at Mr William Baring during disturbances in the Dever valley was found guilty of 'striking Mr William Bingham Baring with a sledgehammer with intent to murder him'. On 30 December, the last day the Commission sat, Cook was brought back to the dock for sentencing and the Judges put on their black caps to pass upon him 'the dreadful sentence of the law.'

Henry Cook was executed in the prison in Jewry Street. On 15 January 1831, he and another condemned man, James Cooper, were awoken at six o'clock and the prison chaplain then stayed with them. Henry Cook spent the time crying. Shortly before eight o'clock, the other prisoners were all assembled to see the 'awful spectacle'. At eight o'clock the prison bell began to toll and the condemned men were escorted to the courtyard at the back of the prison where the gibbet had been prepared. Henry Cook was still sobbing and called out, 'Oh that it should have come to this! Lord, have mercy on me.' Sentence was carried out. Many of the prisoners were openly weeping as they watched. Many would have known these two men all their lives. The bodies were given to the families and buried the same day: Henry Cook, who was only nineteen, now lies in Micheldever churchyard north of Winchester. It was reported that William Bingham Baring, the man he had hit, had done everything in his power to procure a remission of Cook's sentence.

*Scene from the Crimean War in 1854 with the Light Cavalry Brigade charging towards the Russian guns. (Library of Congress, LC-DIG-PPMSCA-05678)*

were signed by 'Captain Swing'. No one knew who had written the letters, but this fictitious Captain Swing became the icon for the movement. Understandably the government and landowners were very worried, and took direct action using their own staff to round up and arrest any rioters who didn't manage to escape.

A Special Commission was convened in Winchester, and met in the Great Hall between 20 and 30 December, with only a two-day break for Christmas. Of all those tried by the Special Commission, 101 were sentenced to death, though only 3 were actually executed, 36 were transported to Australia, 65 were sentenced to hard labour locally, and 67 were acquitted. The authorities were seriously concerned about possible public disorder, explaining why the executions were conducted in the privacy of the prison rather than in public, still the normal practice at that time.

## JOE DUMPER AND THE GUN RIOT – 1908

A Russian gun had been captured during the Crimean War in the 1850s, and presented to the people of Winchester who had it positioned in the Broadway close to King Alfred's statue. It became a popular meeting place for the local Salvation Army and Temperance Association. In 1908, in preparation for the great Winchester Pageant held to raise funds for the work being carried out on the cathedral, the mayor wanted to tidy up the whole area of the Broadway. This included removing some railings and repainting the gun. A rumour sprang up that the gun was to be removed to be scrapped, and a well-known local member of the Salvation Army named Joe Dumper called a meeting to protest, addressing a crowd of about 3,000 from a perch on top of the gun.

The main thread of his argument was that the gun had been presented to the people of the city, and not to the city fathers. The crowd then dragged the gun on its carriage round the city with Dumper on top, and there was a near riot. Clearly there was great public support for the cause, so the militia, who were on stand-by, were not called out. Next day Dumper was made one of 200 Special Constables sworn-in in case of further trouble. He placated the crowd, and the tidy-up was completed in time for the big pageant.

An interesting postscript to this story is that at the beginning of the Second World War the authorities voted to remove the gun, so it could be melted down to aid the war effort. Mindful of the riots thirty years earlier, the council approached Joe Dumper on the subject. An old man by this time, he commented, 'There have been enough arguments. Let them have it.'

# 1914–1945

# TWO WORLD WARS

## THE FIRST WORLD WAR

War broke out in the summer of 1914 and by December the 27th Division of the British Expeditionary Force – around 30,000 men – was stationed at Morn Hill, just east of Winchester, site of a medieval leper hospital. Initially they were under canvas, and many had only recently returned from service in the tropics. It was an exposed location, and the weather was cold. Over this build-up period all their equipment and the machinery of war was assembled. On 19 December the operation to embark the division started. That day the troops marched with all their equipment and horses through the city, up the High Street, and down St Cross Road to Southampton Docks 15 miles away. Many of them would never see England again.

After their departure their camp, by now wooden huts with proper roads, took on a new role as one of the hospitals for casualties returning from the front. In 1918 a branch line was built from Winnall on the Didcot, Newbury and Southampton railway to the three camps in the area; its route can still be seen today as farm tracks. By the end

of the war over 250,000 troops were accommodated in these three main camps in Winchester.

The city was already home to the King's Royal Rifle Corps (KRRC), the Rifle Brigade (RB), and the Hampshire Regiment, and all were based at Peninsula Barracks. Outside the West front of the cathedral are the memorials of the KRRC and the County of Hampshire, and inside are many others. The Rifles still have their regimental headquarters in Winchester, and once a month an officer and a bugler conduct a brief and moving ceremony in the cathedral. After a bugle call, the duty canon offers a prayer and the officer turns the pages of the KRRC and RB Books of Remembrance, reading some of the names from each new page.

Amongst the many army memorials in the cathedral are a few naval ones. A conspicuous one is the bell of HMS *Iron Duke*, Lord Jellicoe's flagship at the Battle of Jutland in 1916, which remained in service until 1948. The bell was placed in the cathedral as a memorial to Admiral Sir Frederic Dreyer, Jellicoe's Flag Captain at Jutland, who 'in a naval career of over fifty years made an outstanding

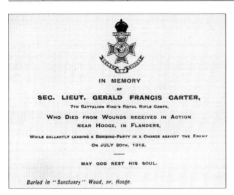

IN MEMORY
OF
**SEC. LIEUT. GERALD FRANCIS CARTER,**
7TH BATTALION KING'S ROYAL RIFLE CORPS,
WHO DIED FROM WOUNDS RECEIVED IN ACTION
NEAR HOOGE, IN FLANDERS,
WHILE GALLANTLY LEADING A BOMBING-PARTY IN A CHARGE AGAINST THE ENEMY
ON JULY 30TH, 1915.

MAY GOD REST HIS SOUL.

Buried in "Sanctuary" Wood, nr. Hooge.

*The King's Royal Rifle Corps was one of the local regiments. Gerald Carter only left school in 1914. (James King)*

contribution to the gunnery of the fleet'. He died in Winchester in 1956.

In the crypt of Winchester Cathedral is a rough wooden cross which originally stood on the Somme battlefield. It is in memory of Lieutenant Valentine Braithwaite MC who died on 1 July 1916, the opening day of the battle. Val had won his Military Cross (one of the first to be awarded in the war) at Mons in 1914. His body was never found and he is commemorated on the Thiepval Memorial. After the war, the original wooden cross was recovered, and placed in the crypt by his uncle, Canon PRP Braithwaite, who was Residentiary Canon of Winchester.

Canon Braithwaite also lost a son in the First World War. Captain Philip Braithwaite, mentioned in despatches and killed during the Battle of Palestine on 23 September 1918, is buried in Haifa military cemetery. During the sixteenth-century reformation, virtually every statue in Winchester Cathedral had been destroyed; Bishop Fox's Chantry Chapel has many niches, some of which would have been filled with small statues. Canon Braithwaite was involved in

plans to replace the missing statues in the 1920s, and donated the statue of Saint George, with the head modelled on a portrait of his son. This is Philip Braithwaite's anonymous memorial in the cathedral, which also remembers the loss of his cousin.

The Battle of the Somme also claimed Lieutenant Colonel the Hon. Guy Victor Baring, son of a distinguished Hampshire banking family and Member of Parliament for Winchester since 1906. He was twice mentioned in despatches, and was killed on 15 September 1916 while commanding the 1st Battalion of the Coldstream Guards. His memorial in the Cathedral South Transept shows him in Guards uniform with a sword below – sadly the original was stolen. He is buried at Fricourt on the Somme.

A lesser known but very beautiful and peaceful memorial is War Cloister in Winchester College. Designed by Sir Herbert Baker, it was dedicated in 1924 and re-dedicated in 1948 as a memorial to Wykehamist dead of two world wars. One of the many names on the walls is 2nd Lieutenant Gerald Francis Carter, a picture of whose memorial card is shown here, and whose only other memorial is on the Menin Gate in Ypres, Belgium. He was a cousin of one of the authors of this book.

## THE SECOND WORLD WAR

The only bombs to hit Winchester directly fell on 9 February 1943. A German bomber was flying north along the line of Jewry Street and its first bomb hit the roof of what is now the Theatre Royal and skidded to a stop at the junction with City Road without exploding. The next exploded by a bus stop in Hyde Street outside a brewery killing seven people who were waiting there; five other bombs dropped in nearby gardens. Mrs Barbara Craze, now mother of a Winchester Blue Badge Guide, was sixteen at the time and on her way to work in Jewry Street; she was thrown to the ground by a passing American GI to protect her! Later that summer a German bomber was shot down having released its bombs about 2 miles south-east of the city. Its pilot parachuted to safety and was arrested and interned. He had been at Winchester College, had left only a year before the start of the war, and was described later as 'such a nice bloke'.

Just east of Winchester is the Matterley Bowl overlooked by Cheesefoot Head. In April 1944, this vast natural amphitheatre was the scene of a major US Army boxing tournament. American and British troops filled the steeply sloping banks of the 'bowl' to see Joe Louis, the heavyweight champion of the world. The venue was also used by General Eisenhower to address the American troops prior to D-Day.

Southwick Park near Portsmouth, then home of the Royal Navy School of Navigation, was the planning base for Operation Overlord – the D-Day landings. Close by in the rural backwater of Droxford Station the Meon Valley Railway had its moment of glory. On Friday, 2 June 1944 a special train arrived amidst great secrecy – it was the Royal Train which had been requisitioned by Winston Churchill as a mobile headquarters. It was parked at Droxford until the evening of 4 June: during his three-day stay major briefings for 'Overlord' were held for Churchill, Allied leaders and military commanders.

The Commonwealth War Graves Commission records a total of 228 burials of war victims in Winchester cemeteries at Magdalen Hill, West Hill, St Giles Hill and St James Hill Roman Catholic cemetery – 158 casualties from the First World War and 70 from the Second World War.

## HAMBONE JUNIOR

In the build-up to D-Day, hundreds of thousands of troops from the Allied Forces were encamped in and around Hampshire's towns, villages, forests and woodland, transforming the whole county into the world's largest military camp. Special bonds were formed between the troops and the local communities. Tanks arriving for the build-up were taken by train to Alresford Station a few miles east of Winchester, en route to various encampments in the area. From 1943 the headquarters of the 47th Infantry Regiment, 9th Division US Army were in Broad Street, Alresford.

Here on the river bank there is a burial stone for their mascot, a dog they called 'Hambone Junior' who had adopted them and was tragically killed in an accident with one of their vehicles in May 1944.

# BIBLIOGRAPHY

Atkinson, Tom, *Elizabethan Winchester* (Faber, 1963)

Beaumont James, Tom, *Winchester* (English Heritage, 2007)

Biddle, Martin, *King Arthur's Round Table* (The Boydell Press, 2000)

Busby, Frederick & Patton, John, *William Walker* (Friends of Winchester Cathedral 2005)

Busby, Frederick, *Saint Swithun* (Friends of Winchester Cathedral, 1997)

Carpenter Turner, Barbara, *A History of the Royal Hampshire County Hospital* (Philimore, 1986)

Carpenter Turner, Barbara, *A History of Winchester* (Philimore, 1992)

Carpenter Turner, Barbara, *The Spanish Match* (Hants Review, July 1954)

Chibnall, Marjorie, *The Empress Matilda* (Blackwell, 1992)

Cook, A.K., *About Winchester College* (Macmillan & Co., 1917)

*Dictionary of National Biography*

Doubleday, H. Arthur & Page, William (Eds), *A History of the County of Hampshire Vol. 2* (1973)

Firth, J. D'E., *Winchester* (Blackie, 1936)

Foxe, John, *The Book of Martyrs*, Revised, with Notes and an Appendix by the Revd William Brawley-Moore (Cassell, Petter & Galpin, c.1880)

Goldsmith, R.F.K, *Military Memorials in Winchester Cathedral* (Winchester Cathedral, 1974)

Hare, John, *Dissolution of the Monasteries in Hampshire* (Hampshire County Council, 1999)

Himsworth, Sheila, *Marriage of Philip II of Spain with Mary Tudor* (Hants Field Club Vol. XXII Part II, 1962)

Hopewell, Peter, *Saint Cross, England's Oldest Almshouse* (Phillimore, 1995)

Hyde Community Archaeology Project, *The Search for Alfred the Great* (Winchester Museums Service, 2005)

Kitchen, G.W., *Historic Towns – Winchester* (Longman, Green, & Co. 1893)

Le Faye, Deirdre (Ed.), *Jane Austen's Letters* (Oxford University Press, 1995)

Macaulay, Lord T.B., *The History of England* (Penguin Classics, 1979 [Originally published 1861])

Marshall, Emma, *Winchester Meads: In the Days of Bishop Ken* (Seeley & Co., 1902)

Milner, John, *The History, Civil and Ecclesiastical & Survey of the Antiquities of Winchester Vol. 1* (1809)

Robertson, Kevin, *The Railways of Winchester*, (Platform 5 Publishing Ltd, 1988)

Rushcombe Foster, E., *The Politics of County Power – Wellington & the Hampshire Gentlemen 1820-52* (Harvester Wheatsheaf, 1990)

Sawyer, Richard, *Civil War in Winchester* (Rowanvale Books, 2002)

Strachan, Isabella, *Emma the Twice Crowned Queen* (Peter Owen Publishers, 2004)

Tomalin, Clare, *Jane Austen, a Life* (Viking, 1997)

Winchester Museums Service, *The Story of the Brooks* (Winchester, 1990)

Wrench, R.G.K., *Winchester Word-Book* (P&G Wells, 1901)